of Christian feasts today. The author finds that these celebrations often stress "a natural or historical meaning that God has long since transcended" in the historical development of the feast. He suggests that the problem of making the Christian liturgy meaningful to non-Western societies is not one of cultural adaptation, since this liturgy, properly understood, has no "cultural resonances" to make its acceptance difficult to non-Western peoples. The problem, rather, is one of formulating a catechesis of this liturgy which will enable its "new resonances," which are "always and everywhere valid," to be heard by anyone who is listening.

By concisely explaining these "new resonances" and the background from which they came, Father Maertens has made a significant contribution to this catechesis. All the members of God's people will be able to profit from his work.

About the Author

Thierry Maertens is widely known for his authoritative work in the fields of biblical and liturgical scholarship. A member of the Benedictine monastery of St. Andrew in Belgium, he is the editor of **Paroisse et Liturgie,** has written scores of books and articles, and has directed such special projects as the highly acclaimed **Bible Missal.** His **The Breath and Spirit of God** was previously published by Fides.

a Feast in Honor of Yahweh

a Feast in Honor of Yahweh

BY THIERRY MAERTENS, O.S.B.

Translated by
Mother Kathryn Sullivan, R.S.C.J.

With a foreword by Eugene H. Maly

FIDES PUBLISHERS, INC. • NOTRE DAME, IND.

In the same series:

THE BREATH AND SPIRIT OF GOD
FEAST IN HONOR OF YAHWEH
MARY, DAUGHTER OF SION
I AM THE WAY
A KING GAVE A MARRIAGE FEAST

Nihil Obstat:
Louis J. Putz, C.S.C.
University of Notre Dame

Imprimatur:
Leo A. Pursley, D.D.
Bishop of Fort Wayne-South Bend

A Feast in Honor of Yahweh *is a translation of* C'est fête en l'honneur de Yahvé, *published in Belgium in 1961 by Desclée de Brouwer.*

Library of Congress Catalog Card Number:
65-13800

Foreword

Some books are worthy of being translated; others need to be. The present volume is in the latter category. In a review that appeared in the *Catholic Biblical Quarterly,* I expressed my enthusiasm for the original edition of Dom Thierry Maerten's book, an enthusiasm that could be said to have contained an implied hope for its translation. Mother Kathryn Sullivan, the very capable co-editor with me of *The Bible Today,* has realized this implied hope in her usual competent way.

Mother Sullivan's fame in the area of original publications may tend to obscure her activity in that of translation. Among her most recent achievements in the latter field are Giblet's *The God of Israel: The God of Christians,* and Gelin's *The Poor of Yahweh.* Risking the indignation of an author who might wish to preserve impartiality with regard to her published works, I would not hesitate to say that *A Feast in Honor of Yahweh* is

Mother Sullivan's most important work of translation. I would like to enlarge on just one reason for that judgment.

As the reader will discover, this volume is a synthesis, beautifully conceived and executed, of work done in various fields: comparative religion, biblical exegesis, biblical theology, and liturgy are among them. While it is not my function to provide here a review of the book, some suggestion of what is contained in it is necessary if I am to jusitfy my enthusiasm. Very briefly, Dom Maertens has traced the evolution of the feasts of biblical religion. Beginning with those elements of pagan antiquity which were adaptable to and adapted by ancient Israel in her worship of the historically intervening God, Dom Maertens has carried his investigation through the many liturgical *aggiornamenti* of the Old Testament period up to the beginnings of Christian worship as sketchily treated in the New Testament. Far from causing any scandal to the reader (the present "openness" of the Church should itself preclude that), the study will make him alert to the totality of a redemptive plan which finds both the elements for its unfolding and the object of its final activity in the real, objective world of man and universe.

This adaptation and subsequent evolution should be especially significant to us today when the members of Christ's Body are undergoing a very real crisis. The crisis is real enough in the objective order where far-reaching changes are being effected not only in the area of liturgy, but also in those of catechetics, the social order, ecumenics. It is even more acute in the subjective order of Christian attitudes. For the great mass of people whose intellectual life never does reach the truly creative level and whose approach to Christian life and worship will be fully determined by the Church's teachers, both lay and cleric, the changes will be unintelligible and meaningless without the proper guidance. And this guidance, as Romano Guardini pointed out in his open letter to the Third German Liturgical Congress, held in April, 1964, must be on the level of education, not of mere instruction. Otherwise, it will simply mean a passage from one meaningless rite or manner of Christian living to another. These people are not to be ignored. Among many of them there is confusion, confusion which can not only lead to the weakening of their faith, but also, perhaps more unfortunately, lead some of the Church's leaders to become wary of the open attitude because of the dangers involved and to close their ranks in a defensive movement.

Educated guidance is therefore essential. And it can obviously be given only by those who themselves have a firm grasp of all that is involved. Here again the subjective crisis manifests itself. It is very difficult for many of the older educators in the Church to change a lifelong pattern of thinkng that has become firmly shaped by constant exercise. Nor is this said in any patronizing attitude. It is said with a deep conviction that a new approach is God's will for the contemporary Church, but with an equally deep respect for the sincere convictions of others. This combination produces a sympathetic understanding of the struggle involved in changing or nuancing those convictions.

Among the younger educators a crisis of another kind is involved. With the majority of them there is already an enthusiastic acceptance of the new approach. For them the danger can be that the forms will be honored while the contents are neglected. Father Gustave Weigel observed, just a few weeks before his death, that the Spirit blows where He will and we must be ready to move with the blowing. In the same vein we can say that it is not enough to blow mightily; we must have the Spirit of truth in our blowing.

In both these cases, it is clear, solid education, pursued in deep faith and with constant adherence to the wise directives of Mother Church, which will supply what is lacking. For the younger ones this means more than an appreciative whiff of all that is brewing. It means a constant steeping of oneself in the brew itself. An enthusiasm that is not solidly grounded will be short-lived and, what is even worse, will cause great havoc in the course of its erratic life. The aura of non-conformity that the new approach in the Church seems to generate is especially attractive to the young. But embracing it is not their challenge. The challenge for them is the steady maturing that only a continuing education, not necessarily formal, can give.

For the older ones this education, similarly achieved through the reading of the best scholars and through participation, where that is possible, in summer institutes or in lecture series, will gradually reveal rich new insights that will more than compensate for the loss of a now outdated defensive approach. And one of the most rewarding insights of this education is a grasp of the role of history both in the unfolding of revelation within the biblical period and in the explicitation and adaptation of that same revelation throughout the Christian centuries. It is amazing to note how God, through the Spirit, has allowed, or better, charged the many forces in history to shape His truth. To note, too, how some periods of history seem to have had more than the normally allotted share of these shaping forces.

Our own period is surely one of these. To live it "to the hilt," and, what is even more exciting, to be an active instrument of the Spirit's blowing, it is necessary to know the divine "system." To know how He has "blown" in the past, to understand how He has made use of even the greatest heresies to build up the Body of Christ, to come to realize that there is never that perfect formula that encapsules all of truth—this is a great part of the divine pedagogy.

This has been, I confess, a rambling introduction. But the final remark does bring me back to the observation that occasioned the ramble. The book that Mother Sullivan here makes available to English-speaking readers is ideally suited for a beginning or, for those already embarked on the new road, a further stimulus in the attaining of that grasp of a God-directed history which is the heart of *aggiornamento*. The area represented in this study is admittedly a limited one. But it is an extremely important one, for it concerns one of the most fundamental acts in the encounter of God and man, the act of worship. If the sovereign Lord can permit the most insignificant or the least esteemed elements of nature and history to shape His worship—and this is, in part, the thesis of Dom Maertens—then we can legitimately conclude that the same providential permission is at work in other areas as well.

It was one of the "constants" in the addresses of the bishops during the sessions of the Council that the Church must be considered in her eschatological dimensions. She must be seen as still struggling to achieve that final goal for which she was founded by the Lord. To achieve this eschatological orientation there is no better school than that of biblical revelation. As he follows the fascinating history of the feasts of ancient Israel, the reader will be carried along in a mighty stream that presses for fulfillment, for an eschatological fulfillment that *was* achieved, in one dimension at least, by the coming of the Christ. We celebrate this fullness in our own Christian liturgy. But that same liturgy will make us more conscious, as we grow in the philosophy of *aggiornamento,* of our own pressing for that full-dimensioned eschatological fulfillment that our Lord will introduce in His second and glorious coming. If this study of Dom Maertens increases that consciousness just one degree, my own enthusiasm will have been amply justified, and we will be able to say with one French reviewer, *Ouvrage vraiment précieux!* And to Mother Sullivan, *Merci mille fois!*

Eugene H. Maly

Mount St. Mary's of the West
Norwood, Ohio

Contents

Introduction

Much has been written about the rites and liturgical feasts of the Jewish people and the relation of their cultic practices to religious observances in the ancient Middle East. Experts in the history of religions have made many studies of such feasts as that of the New Year and never fail to point out that Jewish feasts are in no way deeply original; in fact they resemble pagan feasts in many ways.

In these discussions biblical theology plays no part. Gradually, however, it has become clear that facts in the gospel of John or in the accounts of the Transfiguration or in the story of the Passion, cannot be fully understood without a biblical theology of each and every Jewish feast. But the monographs that have appeared in this area are neither numerous nor well known.

This book attempts to present the principles that biblical theology has established about the feasts recorded in Scripture and in the history of the Chosen People. It also hopes to make these principles better understood and more widely known. It will, in fact, show that the divine pedagogy, through the slow evolution of Jewish feasts towards their end which is Christ, superimposes upon the obvious and natural meaning of each feast new meanings to which the Word alone can give life. A progressive spiritualization of these feasts can be discerned, both in ritual and religious content. By a slow selective process one ritual after another is rejected so that only those that are truly significant prevail. The rites that are retained are precisely those that are eventually incorporated in the Christian cycle.

Our purpose becomes plain. It is the establishment, if possible, of a biblical theology of feasts. The Jewish feast seems to us to be a truly historic fact and at the same time a "biblical theme" in which God's thought becomes more and more explicit as the feast develops. It is this divine thought, discovered in the evolution of the Jewish feasts, that can best reveal the content of our Christian feasts insofar as they complete and perfect the old Jewish feasts.

We shall also move into contemporary pastoral liturgy and ask ourselves whether Christian feasts are presented to the faithful as the prolongation and fulfillment of the dynamism inherent in the evolution of these feasts throughout Scripture. At times we shall be surprised to discover that an emphasis placed today on certain aspects of our feasts may be a regression in the sense that we are stressing a natural or historical meaning that God has long since transcended. The study of the way He has clarified the meaning of the feasts that He has instituted in order to train His people to find a supernatural significance behind the obvious natural meaning will enable us perhaps to draw some valuable lessons for our own catechesis. Lastly, after having observed the step-by-step process of selection evident through the whole course of the evolution of the Jewish feasts, it will be possible to draw some conclusions that can be of value in the difficult modern problem of adapting rites and feasts for new cultures that are now coming into the Church.

Are the feasts that we celebrate and the rites that we practice peculiar to a given civilization, Semitic or Mediterranean? If this be true, can we honestly impose them on peoples of other cultures? But if the divine pedagogy has precisely cleansed these feasts of cultural resonances so as to introduce new resonances that are always and everywhere valid, have we not a serious obligation of introducing these feasts and these rites into every culture, provided that our cathechesis is free from the local conditions of the feasts' Jewish origin, from which they have been emancipated?

Part 1

PAGAN PRELUDES

The time has passed when devout souls are troubled if attempts, often exaggerated, are made to establish parallels between the liturgy of the Jews and that of their pagan neighbors. It is obvious that the Chosen People were pagans before they received Yahweh's special revelation and that they honored their god with feasts and ceremonies similar to those used by their neighbors. It is equally obvious that when it was revealed to the Jews that their God was the true God, unique and personal, they did not overnight invent radically new ceremonies but celebrated, at least at first, "in honor of Yahweh" the feasts that hitherto they had celebrated in honor of some god. Only in the course of time were these ceremonies progressively spiritualized so that they might become what they are now in the Church.

It was therefore in a very human context that the first Jewish feasts began. This fact is essential because it enables us to understand a point of contact between what is human and what is revealed. As a matter of fact, revelation required no new and strictly supernatural rites; it made use of existing rites, purifying them and giving them a new meaning.

Consequently, it will not be superfluous to examine the old feasts of the religious calendars of the Middle East and to discuss their meaning, reminding ourselves before we begin that this was the setting in which the Jews lived and from which they borrowed their own calendars, even though historians still debate certain details.

No attempt will be made to undertake an exhaustive investigation of the religious calendars of those days. Only those elements will be considered that throw light on the origin and final form of the Jewish calendar. We shall not go beyond secondary sources for this part of our study because in them we can find all that we need in order to show the progressive originality, first of the Jewish pattern of feasts, then of the Christian pattern, in relation to the original pagan pattern.

Geographically there are two centers of interest: Sumer with its subsequent civilizations, and Canaan. Abraham was an Aramaean who, even though he knew the true God and left his homeland to follow Him, knew Him in a wholly Sumerian context where such customs as circumcision and child-sacrifice were respected. The religion of Canaan was derived from Sumer and was therefore similar to that of the Hebrews. But while Hebrew rites and feasts became more and more spiritual, those of Canaan remained on the level of nature and even stressed these values. The confrontation of Jewish and Canaanite rites, despite radical inner differences, constituted an unending "temptation" for Israel and one to which the people of God frequently succumbed, precisely because of the external resemblances of the rites. It is a curious fact that Egyptian influence on Israel's religion was slight; our feasts have their origin in the Semitic world.

Culturally, there are also two centers of interest: the nomadic world and the agrarian world. Each of these cultures possessed its own rites. The rhythm of the nomadic world was marked by the worship of the moon, that of the agrarian world by harvest and vintage worship. Sacrifices varied in quality and kind from one world to the other and the contrast between the sacrifice of Abel, a typically nomadic offering, and that of Cain, which was typically agrarian, is indicative of the tension throughout the Middle East between these two cultures and their cultic ramifications. Eventually these differences are reconciled in the religious syncretism of pagan tribes, already accomplished at the moment of the birth of the Hebrew people. But what of the religion of Israel? In it there could be no question of syncretism but of a selection of rites, nomadic or agrarian, made in virtue of a higher norm which we are about to describe.

First, let us examine the principal pagan feasts that mark the temporal divisions of the year.

Chapter One

the Rhythm of Pagan Feasts

A. THE RHYTHM OF ASTRONOMY

1. The New Moon

As early as three thousand years before the birth of Christ most of the religions of the East were regulated according to the lunar cycle.[1] Feast days were usually the day of the new moon (*neomenia*) or the day of the full moon. Moreover, the month began at the moment when the new moon appeared, and reached its summit with the full moon on the fifteenth day. According to the mythological explanation of this lunar rhythm, the moon-god on the last day of the month retired to his nuptial chamber to

[1] Consult on this subject Dhorme, *Les religions de Babylonie et d'Assyrie*; or Charles-Jean, *Le milieu biblique*, v. III.

celebrate a sacred marriage (*hierogamos*) and was born to a new life which was poured down on the earth during the following month. This mythological explanation is interesting because it links the new-moon theme with that of newness of life and fertility. But not much mythology was needed to convince the nomad of the importance of the moon in his personal as well as his clan life and to persuade him to give it place in his religion.

According to this astronomical concept the measuring unit of liturgical time, if one can use the term, is the month. The week was not yet known. The days were numbered from one to thirty, just as they came in the month without any other division. Thus it was the waxing and waning of the moon that determined the time unit.

2. The New Year

The year, unlike the month which had no subdivisions, was composed of twelve months. Perhaps the regular return of the equinoxes led to the establishment of the twelve-month year but it is not unlikely that the cause was a liturgical one. It has been noted that in many regions of the Middle East, tribes were divided into six or twelve groups. Many historians explain that such groupings were formed to ensure the monthly service, tribe by tribe, in the common temple.[2]

2 This explanation is offered even for the division of the Jewish people into twelve tribes. When the different tribal lists are compared, it seems that there were in reality more than twelve tribes. But in every instance an effort was made to prevent the number from exceeding twelve (for example, the tribes of Manasses and Ephraim are some-

In the annual pattern two new-moon services were of paramount importance: that of the seventh month (approximately our month of September) and that of the first month (approximately our month of March). These feasts fall, as can be seen, near the two equinoxes and mark, respectively, the beginning of the decrease and increase of day in relation to night. It is possible that these feasts, in some regions or according to some computations, were also observed as new-year feasts. But it seems fairly certain that in the part of the world which most influenced Israel it was the new moon of the seventh month that was the true new year, although this did not entirely suppress the importance of the new moon of the first month.

In many historical studies the important doctrinal themes of new year celebrations have been analyzed. There is always the danger in studies of this kind of attaching too broad a meaning to a hypothesis by claiming, on very slight evidence, that one has discovered everywhere and always one or another of these themes. There is also the danger of reading into these themes all the deep doctrine that centuries of religious reflection were to introduce gradually into the Israelite world. With these reservations let us present some important themes found in pagan new-year celebrations.

First of all, the theme of *creation*.

---

times united in the single tribe of Joseph). Later these twelve tribes entrusted their cultic privileges to a thirteenth tribe, Levi's, a latecomer to the confederation and one which had no other obligation than the cult.

At the end of the old year the god dies in hell and is at once reborn to a new life in which all who celebrate the new year may share. The coming year is thus a new creation in which the creator-god triumphs once more over the forces of evil and chaos in order to establish his reign of peace and happiness. It is not impossible that some creation epics were read on New Year's day in the Near East, for example, the Sumerian epic of Gilgamesh with its interesting parallels to our first chapter of Genesis.

Then there is the theme of *expiation.*

At the moment of the birth of the new year, its success must not be endangered by any of the preceding year's defilements; they must all be swept away. Therefore this feast is often the occasion of a great temple cleaning and the burning of all that is soiled. Perhaps at times the purification was interior as well as exterior, that is, faults of cultic impurity contracted during the course of the old year were expiated.

There is also the theme of *enthronement.*

Historians have focussed on this theme in their preoccupation with discovering a cultic substructure for some gospel episodes, such as the baptism of Christ or His transfiguration, and for some formulas of the primitive preaching on the dominion acquired by Christ. For the moment let us disregard these hypotheses so as not to lose sight of what is essential. The god, who was reborn to life and who was to preside over the fate of the new year, was officially enthroned. His power over the year was recognized and hopes were expressed that it would bring peace, happiness, and justice. More concretely, the rights and the duties that this enthronement implied were all related to the human king, the incarnation of the god in the midst of the people. Perhaps this custom explains the way the reigns of Hebrew kings were computed in Scripture. It seems that the months from the king's accession until the first new year were counted as one year, and each successive year was dated from new year to new year.

Let us also note the theme of *casting lots* (cf. Est. 3:7-13).

At the beginning of the year the god, to whom the new year was entrusted, was consulted as to the favors or misfortunes that his reign would bring to the people. An effort was made to know his plan for the coming year and to learn what he expected from his subjects.

Lastly, there is a theme of *fertility* that parallels the creation theme.

This is signified mythologically by the sacred marriage of the gods but it is above all an indication of man's concern that the year will bring fruitful harvests, fat flocks, larger families. Each region had its own way of expressing this fertility desire and libations of water poured on the earth must have long been known in lands where, without rain, no fertility was possible.[3]

The new-year feast lasted eight or eleven days. On the

[3] Originally, these libations may have been part of a feast of the first rains or some form of substitute celebration inserted in the autumn New Year feast.

fifth day expiation rites were begun. The temple and the statue of the god were cleansed with a sheep's carcass. Apparently it was believed that all the accumulated impurities of the year were transferred to the animal and disappeared when it was burned or cast into the river or sea. The ceremonies of the last day of the feast were most solemn: a long procession visited the various statues of the gods who were besought by acclamations and noisy cries to draw down on the city the protection of the enthroned god.

3. Conclusion

The liturgy of the ancient Middle East was not satisfied with a cycle of astronomical feasts. Sumer's extensive pantheon must have given rise to many feasts of all kinds. But these purely idolatrous feasts left no trace on the religion of Israel and they can be ignored here. As for the astronomical feasts it is important to grasp their orientation and, if the term be permitted, their spiritual meaning. Mythology apart—and it seems that this element was not so essential that the Jews could eventually disregard it—the feasts of the astronomical order honored the order of the created world, the regular rhythm of its evolution, man's submission to the dominion of "the elements of the world" as Paul was to say later. Here we find ourselves in the heart of a natural religion where man is aware of his solidarity with the elements of creation and makes this very solidarity the object of his praise and prayer.

B. THE RHYTHM OF ASTROLOGY

The domain we are now considering is an artificial one. Here the order of man's worship is not dictated by nature's laws but by the computations of human intelligence, especially by the magicians of the period. Analyzing and minutely determining the astronomical rhythm, these magicians discovered new and unsuspected laws that they promulgated in a thousand and one precepts which would make it possible for man to act according to the plan intended for him by one or another star, one or another god. The research of these magicians revealed days of good or bad omen which had to be respected if man wished to maintain his solidarity with the rhythm of creation. We will not involve ourselves in their lists of prescriptions or be concerned about their mathematical laws in which are found a mixture of number-symbolism, some magic, and much mythology. All this is not closely related to worship as such and corresponds rather to the daily horoscope printed in newspapers. For example, on the ninth day of the month, to sweep the house or wash one's feet would bring bad luck. Each day had its own prohibitions according to the caprice of one of the gods.

Yet it is interesting that among these lucky and unlucky days, there is one group that was to have important religious consequences. This group of days contained multiples of seven: the seventh, fourteenth, twenty-first, eighteenth, and nineteenth days.[4] On those days almost

[4] The nineteenth day of the month no doubt was unlucky because it was considered to be a multiple of seven (the forty-ninth day [7x7]

everyone was obliged "to do nothing" (*sabbatu,* in Acadian).

Here is a typical astrological precept:

> The shepherd of the peoples [i.e., the king] must not eat meat cooked over coals, he must not eat bread baked under ashes, he must not change his clothes, he must not put on clean garments, he must not offer sacrifice. The king must not go out in his chariot nor exercise his sovereign power. The diviner must not deliver oracles in the place of mystery. The doctor must not touch a patient. This is not a suitable day to undertake a project.

For the nineteenth day there is this additional note:

> This day is unlucky for anything that doctors want to do.

Several characteristics of these days deserve to be mentioned. In a style surprisingly like that of our modern horoscopes a prohibition of work is put first. This is important. The enforced rest is not considered as a form of natural repose: this or that is forbidden lest it affect the star that controls and protects these actions. It is the fear of violating a taboo that prevails. Moreover, these prohibitions have no connection with worship. The rest that is imposed is an act of magic rather than a truly religious rite. Actually religion is so dissociated from such acts that the horoscope forbids offering sacrifice or consulting diviners on these days.

At first the set of seven unlucky days had no significance as a measure of time. The month and not the week

---

after the first day of the month was the nineteenth day of the next month). This is of course highly artificial but the symbolism of numbers played at times an important role in the composition of liturgical calendars and must be kept in mind and evaluated.

was the time unit. But it cannot be denied that we are at the beginning of a series of purifications that lead to the Jewish Sabbath. These will be noted later. The act of purification, in fact, was begun in the pagan world, if we can judge by the prescriptions of Lagos in 2500 B.C. Despite the text cited above, these days were sanctified by the offering of sacrifice. Very quietly the magic number seven becomes a liturgical number.

The astrological rhythm of seven is a by-product of the natural rhythm of the month and years. It is the fruit of computation and magic expressing itself most especially in a religion of fear and terror in which man tried to shelter himself from the wrath of the gods and to conform to their caprices. If there is anything religious in such an attitude, it can be questioned whether this element is in any way cultic.

C. THE RHYTHM OF AGRARIANISM

1. General Remarks

Especially in Canaan, Israel was to discover or re-discover the rhythm of agrarian feasts. We do not know whether Israel lived according to a strictly agrarian rhythm in Egypt. In any event it is certain that it was not an Egyptian agrarian rhythm that provided Israel with inspiration but rather a rhythm that was Semitic in origin and that was found in Canaan at the time of the Israelite installation there. In Egypt, in fact, the new year began three months earlier. There the time unit seems to have been the decade and the lunar rhythm was supplanted by the life of the Nile itself. Jewish liturgy reveals no trace of Egyptian influence. When Israel was in Goshen it probably kept its own calendar and observed its own agrarian feasts. We may even suppose that this gave rise to incidents between Israelites and Egyptians and it is possible that one of the first incidents between Pharaoh and Moses involved a question of a liturgical calendar:

> Then you and the elders of Israel shall go to the king of Egypt and say to him: The Lord, the God of the Hebrews, has sent us word. Permit us, then, to go a three days' journey in the desert, that we may offer a sacrifice to the Lord, our God. Yet I know that the King of Egypt will not allow you to go unless he is forced. . . (Ex. 3:18-19).

By way of contrast, as soon as the Chosen People entered Canaan they discovered agrarian feasts with which they were in perfect accord. These customs, it is true, are found in other lands as well as in Canaan, but it is difficult to understand their essential characteristics without consulting the Bible, which is ultimately the most important document that we possess on the agrarian feasts of the ancient Middle East. In our later biblical investigation we will note significant details of pagan agrarian feasts. Here we can give only a rapid sketch.

First of all, it should be observed that religious syncretism had already combined certain feasts when Israel conquered the Promised Land. Thus it was that two major agrarian feasts were celebrated, one in the first month (the feast of the Harvest) and one in the seventh month (the feast of Tents). There was also a third feast, at that time less important; it was celebrated in the third month and on that day was offered the first sheaf of wheat. The observance of these two major agrarian feasts in the first and seventh months was in accord with the old astronomical rhythm where these two months, especially the latter, were of great importance. As a result the characteristics of the agrarian and astronomical feasts of the new year were blended, a process already completed when Israel entered Canaan. From our point of view this syncretism is significant because it combined elements belonging to the agrarian order with astronomic elements belonging to the nomadic order. We shall see that the Hebrews did not do this when they combined the elements of their feasts.

A second and significant characteristic of these agrarian feasts is that they are all based on the harvest or the gathering of fruit. These are essentially feasts of wealth. The peasant, the typical worker of that day, records the results of his work, stores his riches in barns and joyfully proclaims the success that is his in the fertility of compliant nature. At the same time he recognizes that his Baal, the god of the power of nature, is responsible for this fertility and as a touch of gratitude he offers him the first fruits of his abundance. His understanding goes even deeper. Having shared in the fertility his god has given him, he offers him a banquet in the temple, in which the god and his client share these fruits in "a communion sacrifice." It is characteristic of these feasts, especially the feast of the seventh month, that they are prolonged by banquets, drinking bouts, rejoicing, and innumerable dances in which the quantity of refreshments is measured by the wealth harvested. This note of agricultural abundance and thanksgiving is important in the light of the spiritualization that the theology of Israel will effect.

If we are to transpose into modern form the "mystique" of these feasts, we willingly acknowledge that they hymn man's joy in possessing the earth through his work, in knowing that he is the master of nature, and that he derives his happiness from his real share in his god's fructifying work. We might almost say that these ancient feasts contain "a theology of work."

2. The Feast of the First Sheaf

Let us note some special characteristics of each of these agrarian feasts. The essential rite of the first feast is the presentation to the god of the first sheaf of barley found in the fields. This is a relatively more serious celebration than that of the seventh month: work now presses and there is no leisure for a week of merry-making such as will be welcome in the seventh month. A curious rite of unleavened bread has become part of this feast of the first month. In connection with the new year we said that an effort was made to purify the temple of all that was soiled or that recalled the preceding year, now considered to be dead and unable to influence the new year. A similar train of thought explains the use of unleavened bread. In those days dough was mixed with fermented flour. When new grain was available the question was whether to use yeast with it that was made from flour belonging to last year's harvest. Would this not "mix the spirits" as the Bantus say today? So unleavened bread was eaten until the new flour had fermented and new yeast was ready. Meanwhile, every effort was made to throw away all traces of old leaven just as the children still do in devout Jewish families.

3. The Feast of the Sheaf of Wheat

The second feast has long been obscure; it is rarely mentioned in the pagan world of those days. On this feast the first blades of wheat were offered in the temple, shortly after the presentation of the first sheaves of barley. In the beginning, this feast was probably not celebrated exactly at the third month and it is even less likely that this was exactly fifty days after the offering of the barley sheaf. These were later modifications that we will be able to understand within the spiritual context of the Jewish world.

4. The Feast of Harvests

Even in pagan times this was the most important feast of the year. It had something in common with the feast of the New Year in the seventh month. During the gathering of fruit and grapes, to save time, it was customary for the workers to move into temporary huts, just substantial enough to shelter them while they were busy with the harvest. It was in this setting of hastily erected shelters that the banquets and the merry-making of the agrarian feast of the seventh month took place.

D. A MAGICAL NOMADIC RITE

One last pagan feast must be mentioned. This was a nomadic rite which could be observed during any season of the year and was at first connected with no special feast. Its original meaning was magical, not cultic. To protect tent-dwellers from a cataclysm or an epidemic, a lamb was strangled and its blood was poured on the tent-poles. This was a magical gesture but absolutely classic and frequently found in primitive religions. Today it is still used by many Bedouin tribes and by some Bantu clans. The lamb is not necessarily eaten. If there is a meal it has no religious significance. The blood alone has preservative power and prevents the entrance of the evil spirit and the destroying angel. It is important to recall that at this early stage the rite was not connected with any feast but might be performed whenever danger threatened.

E. CONCLUSION

We have briefly summarized the pagan beginnings of the Jewish liturgical year, basing our remarks not on primary sources but on the works of specialists. Our aim has simply been to discover the context in which spiritualization of the Hebrews took place. In fact, by limiting ourselves to the feasts and rites destined to have repercussions in the religion of the Jews, we have so singularly purified and spiritualized the pagan religion of Sumer and Canaan that we have not considered the directly idolatrous feasts so frequently found in their calendars.

It is much to Israel's credit that it was able from the first to select from the common patrimony of the Middle East what was best able to express its own religion.

From the feasts that we have examined we have seen that feasts of both nomadic and agrarian origin had been happily combined at the moment when Israel itself had come to the end of its nomadic life and had entered the land that it was now to cultivate as farmers. From the nomadic rhythm, came the feasts of the new moon, the new year, and the strangled lamb rite. From the agrarian rhythm, came the feasts of the offering of first fruits of field and vineyard, feasts of harvest followed by merry-making. A third rhythm, more artificial than these, was that of the septenaries of unlucky days.

Apparently these combined feasts were not accepted without some difficulty by the Jews. Echoes may be detected in Israel's reaction to Canaanite agrarian feasts. In any case, the nomadic feasts were much more serious than the agrarian feasts and more easily spiritualized.

It may be that the old account of Cain and Abel acquired additional meanings in the course of later re-readings, and testifies to the opposition between nomadic and agrarian rites and feasts. In it may be found the expression of God's will manifest in a form of "competition" between the two types of sacrifice, a competition in which the nomadic sacrifice was declared superior:

> Now Abel was a keeper of flocks and Cain a tiller of the soil. In the course of time Cain brought to the Lord an offering of the fruit of the ground. Abel also brought some of

> the firstlings of his flock with their fat portions. The Lord was pleased with Abel and his offerings; but for Cain and his offering he had no regard (Gen. 4:2-5).

Whatever be the rhythm of the pagan feasts, nomadic or agrarian, they reveal two very different spiritual attitudes. The nomad is full of fear. He is afraid of his god and seeks to conciliate him. He looks on a feast as a means of achieving harmony with nature, adapting to its rhythms with as little difficulty as possible, avoiding all causes of disturbance. When nature is hostile, he shields himself from danger with the rite of protective blood. The man who cultivates the soil, on the contrary, has greater self-confidence. He sings the praises of his work and offers it proudly to his god. He is rich, and the nomad seems to be poor. While the nomad tries to live in harmony with the laws of nature, the farmer rejoices over the control of nature by his work. The former is passive, the latter is active. The former is more interior, the latter needs to express himself, to rejoice more, to dance and to offer holocausts.

These are only psychological traits which we should not make too much of, lest we force meanings not true at that time. But it is valuable, at the beginning of our investigation, to attempt to define these two mentalities, the nomadic and the agrarian, because we will see that they are the two poles in the evolution of Jewish liturgy and will have repercussions upon Christian liturgy.

Part II

FROM JEWISH FEASTS TO CHRISTIAN FEASTS

Two forms of exposition are possible here. We could study all the feasts in a given period, analyze their contents, then move from period to period, noting new characteristics. Or, we could trace each feast through the centuries, synthesizing our findings only at the close of the last analysis. We prefer the second formula. It is easier to follow the development of a feast rather than to analyze the feasts of a given period. All feasts did not evolve at the same time. A certain period significant in the development of one feast might be without meaning in the development of another. The method we have chosen is certainly more analytic but it will be more profitable and enable us to draw more solid conclusions.

It is important to observe that in her liturgical feasts Israel was amazingly faithful to human rites and feasts, excepting, of course, anything idolatrous. We shall see that the Jewish religion crystalized around feasts that the Chosen People had received from their neighbors; nothing new was added until the last years (the feast of the dedication of the temple, Purim, etc.). In other words, revealed religion felt no need to invent new rites or new feasts. It merely accepted, purified, and progressively spiritualized existing feasts. This also explains the bonds of continuity between the human and the Christian feast, despite the magnitude of the new contents. The supernatural and the revealed do not break with the natural but are inscribed in a mysterious continuity made of transcendence and also of fidelity.

It should also be observed that Jewish liturgy is extremely careful in this selective process. A feast that has come down to us has had to pass a whole series of increasingly exacting tests. Is it able to express the nomadic experience? Will it later be able to express the historic experience of God's salvation? Will it be able to make this salvation present, at least in its moral exigencies? Will it be able to contain the people's hope for the eschatological renewal of salvation? Lastly, will it be able to define the person of Christ Himself achieving man's salvation through His acceptance of the Father's will? Our Christian feasts have successfully met the demands of this series of purifications. Therefore we must also experience these same purifications interiorly so as to move on the plane of these feasts and thus attain their new object.

Following these guiding principles we will trace the evolution of Jewish liturgical feasts and see how they reach their final and perfect form in Christianity.

Chapter Two

Feasts of the New Moon

A. THE PAGAN OBSERVANCE

There can be no doubt that the primitive Jewish calendar adopted the Sumerian new-moon feasts. There is not much information about this custom and few texts afford a theology of these feasts, but we can glean a number of lessons from extant early documents.

The oldest text on this subject locates the episode of David's flight from Saul's court in the context of a new-moon feast. Here are the significant details:

> And Jonathan said to David: Whatsoever thy soul shall say to me, I will do for thee. And David said to Jonathan: Behold tomorrow is the new moon, and I according to custom am wont to sit beside the king to eat. Let me go then that

> I may be hid in the field till the evening of the third day. If thy father look and inquire for me, thou shalt answer him: David asked me that he might run to Bethlehem his own city: because there are solemn sacrifices there for all his tribe. If he shall say: It is well: thy servant shall have peace. But if he be angry, know that his malice is come to its height. Deal mercifully then with thy servant: for thou hast brought me thy servant into a covenant of the Lord with thee. But if there be any iniquity in me, do thou kill me, and bring me not in to thy father. And Jonathan said: Far be this from thee: for, if I should certainly know that evil is determined by my father against thee, I could do no otherwise than tell thee. . . . So David was hid in the field. And the new moon came: and the king sat down to eat bread. And when the king sat down upon his chair (according to custom) which was beside the wall, Jonathan arose; and Abner sat by Saul's side; and David's place appeared empty. And Saul said nothing that day: for he thought it might have happened to him, that he was not clean, nor purified. And when the second day after the new moon was come, David's place appeared empty again. And Saul said to Jonathan his son: Why cometh not the son of Isai to meat neither yesterday nor today? And Jonathan answered Saul: He asked leave of me earnestly to go to Bethlehem. And he said: Let me go, for there is a solemn sacrifice in the city. One of my brethren hath sent for me: and now if I have found favor in thy eyes, I will go quickly, and see my brethren. For this cause he came not to the king's table . . . (1 Kgs. 20:4-29).

We can draw several facts from this text. Two rites dominated the celebration of the new moon. First, there was a meal repeated on two consecutive days. Apparently a certain ceremonial was observed on this occasion because reference is made to places reserved for the guests who were expected to be in a state of ritual purity. This explains how Saul accounted for David's absence on the first day. Secondly, the celebration of the new moon also required the offering of a clan sacrifice; it was believed that David had attended one of these. Apparently the banquet was a meal of comunion with God and it may have been eaten in the temple. Probably the ceremonial had not changed much since pagan days; the only difference was that it was now celebrated "in honor of Yahweh" instead of as a hierogamous mystery. This monotheistic modification is important, but the ceremony itself remained pagan and it is possible that, despite the ritual purity required of those who were present at these banquets, they were often the occasion of all kinds of excesses that were most unreligious. In any event the characteristic note that is found in all the Old Testament prophetic texts referring to new moons is a condemnation of their excesses and formalism.

> When you come in to visit me, who asks these things of you? Trample my courts no more! Bring no more worthless offerings; your incense is loathsome to me. New moon and sabbath, calling of assemblies, octaves with wickedness: these I cannot bear. Your new moons and festivals I detest; they weigh me down, I tire of the load. When you spread out your hands, I close my eyes to you; though you pray the more, I will not listen. Your hands are full of blood! Wash yourselves clean! Put away your misdeeds from before my eyes; cease doing evil; learn to do good. Make justice your aim: redress the wronged, hear the orphan's plea, defend the widow. Come now, let us set things right, says the Lord: though your sins be like scarlet, they may become white as snow; though they be crimson red, they may become white as wool. If you are willing, and obey, you shall eat the good things of the land; but if you refuse and resist, the sword shall consume you: for the mouth of the Lord has spoken (Is. 1:12-20).

From this text it is clear that the new moon is among other things, an occasion when men cross the temple court to offer sacrifices. The prophets ask that the feast be spiritualized so that the sacrifice be a sign of a converted heart. Let us also note in the last verse an allusion to a pagan purpose of the feast. The new moon was offered to assure the regular rhythm of the earth's fruitfulness and harvests (". . . you will eat the good things of the land"). From now on this seasonal rhythm will depend on conversion of heart.

The prophet Amos delivered a similar invective when he described thieves impatiently waiting the end of the new-moon rest so that they could resume their dishonest work:

> "When will the New Moon be over," you ask, "that we may sell our grain, and the Sabbath, that we may display the wheat? We will diminish the epha, add to the shekel, and fix our scales for cheating!" (Amos 8:5).

Here, as well as in the preceding text, may be seen the ideological connection between new moons and the fruits of the earth. New moons were meant to be days of thanksgiving to God for the rhythm of nature. But men became so preoccupied with amassing profits that they forgot to give thanks.

Osee's words are equally significant:

> Since she has not known that it was I who gave her the grain, the wine, and the oil, and her abundance of silver and gold, which they used for Baal, therefore I will take back my grain in its time, and my wine in its season; I will snatch away my wool and my flax, with which she covers her

> nakedness. . . . I will bring to an end all her joy, her feasts, her new moons, her Sabbaths, and all her solemnities (Osee 2:8-13).

It is interesting to observe that in Osee as well as in Isaias, God's sanction against the formalism of the new-moon celebrations will take the form of shattering the regularity of the harvest cycle: "I will take back my grain in its time." . . . "If you are willing, and obey, you shall eat the good things of the land." This would seem to indicate that even as late as the years before the Exile new moons celebrated the regular rhythm of nature which was assured by the normal return of the moon, as well as man's perfect harmony with the elements of the world. It should also be observed that the prophets wished this same harmony to exist between man's will and God's will.

B. NEW MOONS AND THE NEW CREATION

Jewish new moons, like pagan new moons, were celebrations in honor of the order and regularity of creation. But the reverses of the Exile were a partial interruption of this order. Man with his heart of stone is no longer the perfect image of God. A new man must be re-created and God must give him a heart of flesh. Man's sin has disturbed even the laws of nature. Therefore, a new creation will be made:

> Lo, I am about to create new heavens and a new earth; the things of the past shall not be remembered or come to mind. Instead, there shall always be rejoicing and happiness in what I create . . . (Is. 65:17-18).

The author has just anounced a new creation; logically, he also tells of a new form of worship that will celebrate this new creation month by month:

> As the new heavens and the new earth which I will make shall endure before me, says the Lord, so shall your race and your name endure. From one new moon to another, and from one Sabbath to another, all mankind shall come to worship before me, says the Lord (Is. 66:22-23).

This new creation will be marked by the regularity of obedient hearts to God's plan and not merely by the obedience of exterior elements to divine providence. These new-moon celebrations thus become the sign of man's submission to the Covenant and the occasion of the renewal of this Covenant. Trito-Isaias completes and spiritualizes what Isaias, Amos, and Osee had begun. In this new perspective new moons and sabbaths are named in the same texts and both are signs of the covenant that establishes the new creation.[1]

The post-exilic legislative texts give few details but are careful to locate the lunar feasts on this new plane. Ezechiel specifies in his Torah that an exception is to be made to the rule that sacred things must be protected from profane eyes: therefore a door is to be opened in the temple for the Prince. Through this door the people may look but not enter so that they can see all that takes place and prostrate themselves before Yahweh (Ez. 46:1-7).

1 After Osee 2:13, lunar feasts and sabbaths are united in prophetic texts. Does this not indicate that these feasts gradually lost their distinctive characteristics and became a kind of "superogatory sabbath" that could easily be included in the mystique of the sabbath covenant? Cf. *infra*, p. 152.

This is perhaps all that remains of the old sacred banquet taken by the king and his guests in the temple at the first moon. This prescription then became part of the sacerdotal law:

> On the first of each month you shall offer as a holocaust to the Lord two bullocks, one ram, and seven unblemished yearling lambs, with three tenths of an epha of fine flour mixed with oil as the cereal offering for each bullock, two tenths of an epha of fine flour mixed with oil as the cereal offering for the ram, and one tenth of an epha of fine flour mixed with oil as the cereal offering for each lamb, that the holocaust may be a sweet-smelling oblation to the Lord. Their libations shall be half a hin of wine for each bullock, a third of a hin for the ram, and a fourth of a hin for each lamb. This is the new-moon holocaust for every new moon of the year (Num. 28:11-15).

Thus despite the abuses that defiled the celebration of lunar feasts before the Exile, the prophets had no desire to condemn them. On the contrary, they tried to preserve and spiritualize them. Nehemias did not hesitate to include them in the calendar of feasts for the new Jerusalem community (Neh. 10:33-34). But we should not believe too quickly that the people always thought of these feasts on the new spiritual plane.

Later[2] we shall speak of the perpetual solar calendar which was established after the Exile, and which profoundly influenced the last stages of the evolution of Jewish feasts. Possibly this calendar was responsible for the neglect of the feasts of the lunar calendar. In this way, before the coming of Christ, feasts were discarded that

2 (See p. 115).

were too strictly astronomical to share in the evolution of the other feasts.

C. FREED FROM THE ELEMENTS OF THE WORLD

Let us summarize Old Testament teaching on the subject of lunar feasts by saying that they preserved the bond between man and the regular rhythm of the order of creation. They might be called feasts of Noah's covenant (Gen. 9:12). Jews felt no shame in observing these feasts in the manner of their pagan neighbors. Yet they made several attempts to spiritualize their celebration: first, because they wished to incorporate them in an exclusively monotheistic cult; then because they wished to be able to observe them with sincerity; lastly because they wished to make them signs of the new creation of hearts and wills.

Yet when the new creation was truly understood in the New Testament, there was no question of observing these feasts. Two unmistakable texts of Paul abrogated them. His reasons are worth close study:

> Now I say, as long as the heir is a child . . . he is under guardians and stewards until the time set by his father. So we, too, when we were children, were enslaved under the elements of the world. But when the fullness of time came, God sent His Son, born of woman, born under the Law, that he might redeem those who were under the Law, that we might receive the adoption of sons. And because you are sons, God has sent the Spirit of his Son into our hearts, crying, "Abba, Father." So that he is no longer a slave, but a son; and if a son, an heir also through God. But then in-

> deed, not knowing God, you served those who really are not gods. But now that you have come to know God, or rather to be known by God, how is it that you turn again to the weak and beggarly elements, which you desire to serve again? You are observing days and months and seasons and years. I fear for you, lest perhaps I have labored among you in vain (Gal. 4:1-11).

According to Paul, therefore, as long as man was dependent on "the elements of this world" (that is, the stars), he belonged to the order of natural creation and could "observe the months" (that is, the lunar feasts). But an ontological change has taken place: man is not only a man, he has become a new creature, a son of God belonging to a new plan of creation that is not bound by the laws and the elements of the old creation. To return to the new-moon celebrations, especially in a pagan world unaware of the Israelite spiritualization of these feasts, would be to deny the change effected in us by Christ; it would mean to seek recreation with slaves when one has become a son of the family.

In another letter Paul uses a similar argument:

> Let no one, then, call you to account for what you eat or drink or in regard to a festival or a new moon or a Sabbath. These are a shadow of things to come, but the substance is of Christ. Let no one cheat you who takes pleasure in self-abasement and worship of the angels, and enters vainly into what he has not seen, puffed up by his mere human mind. Such a one is not united to the head, from whom the whole body, supplied and built up by joints and ligaments, attains a growth that is of God (Col. 2:16-19).

It is not the "growth" of the moon that we should celebrate but the "growth" of the Body of Christ which derives nourishment and unity from its Head. Paul concludes with these admirable words:

> If you have died with Christ to the elements of the world, why, as if still living in the world, do you lay down the rules: "Do not touch; nor taste; nor handle!" (Col. 2:20-21).

The theme of Christian liberty provides the foundation of Paul's thought. Christ has freed us from sin, as well as from the law and the elements of the world. Therefore the lunar feasts that might have been the celebration of the regular rhythm of these elements of the world, that might even have been the expression of the expectation of this new creation, are obviously incapable of signifying this freedom because they suppose, on the contrary, our enslavement to the elements of a world to which we no longer totally belong.

We see, then, in regard to these celebrations the "selective spiritualization" of which we spoke above. Certain feasts were able, for a time, to obey this law and adapt themselves to its demands, but a moment came when they were unable to change their meaning any further, so they could only disappear. It will be a basic law of the new Christian liturgy to draw feasts and rites from the order of creation but only insofar as they are able to express our freedom in regard to this creation. A feast of creation which is unable also to signify the new creation in the liberty of the children of God has no place in Christian liturgy. It is no longer the increase of natural elements that we should celebrate but the growth of the Son of God in us, in the Person of Christ.

Chapter Three

the New Year

The New Year feast is in fact only a new-moon feast more solemn than all the rest. Will it survive where they have failed, or has it characteristics all its own that will enable it to continue with new meaning? This is the question that we shall try to answer in this paragraph. Let us begin by pointing out that, even in the pagan world, the feast of the New Year was combined with the harvest feasts of the seventh month. As a result, some elements of these feasts seem to have become part of the New Year feast, others of the harvest feast. The elements in the New Year feast that we choose to examine here are not necessarily complete. The next section will contain the needed complementary material.[3] Here we shall limit ourselves

[3] See p. 62.

to the characteristic elements of the first day of the seventh month. They are to be found in two important Old Testament texts (Num. 29:1-6; Lev. 23:23-25). These texts are late, probably postexilic, whatever be the date of the material they reproduce. This explains the hypothesis of some historians[4] that the New Year did not become an independent feast until after the Exile. Earlier it had been included in a general way in "the" feast of the seventh month of which we shall next speak. It must have been the work of the priests to disengage the lines of each rite of this feast, the better to establish its time and meaning. So it was the priestly reform that divided the feast into three distinct parts: on the first day, the feast of Acclamations or the New Year; on the tenth day, the feast of Expiation; from the fifteenth to the twenty-second, the feast of Tents.

A. THE DAY OF SHOUTING

Bible and Mishna agree that the first day of the seventh month was the day of "acclamations"—or the day of the "shouters," or the day of "trumpets." Biblical translations should agree about the vocabulary of this feast. Originally it opened with the blowing of the trumpet (*terou'a*). These instruments proclaimed to the whole city that the new moon had appeared so that there might be no disagreements about calendars or calculations. Trumpets sounded for all liturgical feasts (cf. Num.

[4] This hypothesis is defended by Mowinckel, *Palmenstudien, II* and by Morgenstern, *The Three Calendars of Ancient Israel.* Hebr. Un. Coll. 1924, 13-78, and 1926, 77-107.

10:10) but special importance was attached to their blaring at the beginning of each new year. Instruments for the measurement of time were in those days highly experimental and sometimes inaccurate. A whole treatise of the Talmud is devoted to the ways the new moon should be determined and how the elders or priests should be informed so that they can be responsible for blowing the trumpets.[5]

Once the trumpets were heard, the Jews shouted loudly and long in order to give a noisy welcome to the beginning of the new year. When some translations of the Bible speak of the "shouters," they are referring to the blare of the trumpets and the acclamations of the crowd.

This is a wholly human rite to designate the time and to communicate this officially to the people by means of trumpets. The priestly texts agree:

> On the first day of the seventh month you shall hold a sacred assembly, and do no sort of work; it shall be a day on which you sound the trumpet (Num. 29:1).
> The Lord said to Moses, "Tell the Israelites: On the first day of the seventh month you shall keep a sabbath rest, with a sacred assembly and with the trumpet blasts as a reminder" (Lev. 23:23-24).

Yet we cannot restrict the religious significance of the day of acclamations to the official proclamation of a new chronological period. The *terou'a* has a very special meaning in Israel which we cannot neglect here.

5 Edition Schwab, *Rosch Haschana,* VI.

In early times the word *terou'a* denoted the cry, like the rolling of thunder, that was raised when the ark of Yahweh the Warrior was carried to victory. This Hebrew battle cry was powerful enough to shatter the walls of Jericho (Jos. 6:5-21). This war cry also became a religious cry when it was raised in honor of the Ark of the Covenant, the throne of Yahweh the King (1 Kgs. 17: 20; 4:5-8; 2 Kgs. 6:15). Many psalms allude to the liturgical acclamations that accompany Yahweh's enthronement:

> All you peoples, clap your hands, shout to God with cries of gladness, for the Lord, the Most High, the awesome, is the great king over all the earth. . . . God mounts his throne amid shouts of joy; the Lord, amid trumpet blasts. Sing praise to God, sing praise; sing praise to our king; sing praise (Ps. 46:1-7).
>
> Sing joyfully to God our strength; acclaim the God of Jacob. Take up a melody and sound the timbrel, the pleasant harp and the lyre. Blow the trumpet at the full moon, on our solemn feast (Ps. 80:2-4).

This last text is interesting because it associates the royal theme of trumpets with the shouters of the New Year feast, in fact with all the lunar feasts. Thus the acclamation rite of the first day of the seventh month is not only a rite that regulates time but is also a means of affirming Yahweh's dominion over time. This was the only spiritualization of New Year's day: to the Israelites it meant Yahweh's royal entrance and the flight of all their enemies just as their adversaries had once fled before the Ark of the Covenant.

B. THE ANNOUNCEMENT OF THE NEW EON

The New Testament shows more respect for this day than for any of the other lunar feasts. We must pause to explain this.

Luke's attitude is to be noted first. He refers to the acclaim made when Jesus entered Jerusalem:

> And when he was drawing near, being by now at the descent of the Mount of Olives, the whole company of the disciples began to rejoice and to praise God with a loud voice for all the miracles that they had seen (Lk. 19:37).

We shall see below[6] how Christ's entrance into Jerusalem was for Him and His disciples a true celebration of the feast of the seventh month. The cries of the people correspond to the cries of the New Year liturgy, inaugurating a unique and never-ending new year, a year of divine grace opening directly into eternity. Thus the true Christian new year is not concerned with the regular renewal of the year. We have escaped from creation's cyclic rhythm. Our new year opened in the presence on earth of the First-born of all creatures who brought men His seed of immortality and eternity.

For this reason the "shouters" are not heard in the church's liturgy but they will be heard when the new year of the eternal and divine economy will begin in all its fullness on the Lord's Day. Trumpets and cries will play an important role in the apocalyptic inaugural of eternity:

> But immediately after the tribulation of those days, the sun will be darkened, and the moon will not give her light, and

[6] See p. 80.

> the stars will fall from heaven, and the powers of heaven will be shaken. And then will appear the sign of the Son of Man in heaven. . . . And he will send forth his angels with a trumpet and a great sound, and they will gather his elect from the four winds, from one end of the heavens to the other (Mt. 24:29-31).

Notice in this text the clear allusion to the perishability of the "elements of the world" that were involved in the lunar and New Year celebrations: sun, moon, stars will lose their brightness. The trumpets will not disappear for they will call the elect to the beginning of a new year that will never end:

> A trumpet, too, will announce the coming of the Lord's Day. For the Lord himself with cry of command, with voice of archangel, and with trumpet of God will descend from heaven. . . . But of the times and seasons, brethren, you have no need that we write to you, for you yourselves know well that the day of the Lord is to come as a thief in the night (1 Thess. 4:16-5:2).

John gives a detailed preview of the feast of shouters that will be the prelude to eternity. Seven trumpets sound (Apoc. 8-11) and after the seventh the shouts of the elect are heard:

> And the seventh angel sounded the trumpet; and there were loud voices in heaven saying, "The kingdom of this world has become the kingdom of our Lord and of his Christ, and he shall reign forever and ever." . . . And the temple of God in heaven was opened, and there was seen the ark of his covenant in his temple, and there came flashes of lightning, and peals of thunder, and an earthquake, and great hail (Apoc. 11:15-19).

Thus the ancient *terou'a* that accompanied the Ark is raised once again around the new heavenly ark. It rings out as thunder rolls and trumpets blare. The last new year has begun and it will never end.[7]

So we see that the New Testament does not purely and simply reject the feast of the New Year but gives it an eschatological dimension. It is no longer celebrated, because the Church already has entered upon a year that has no end. Yet the feast of acclamation will be observed once more, not in expectation but in fullness of light and totally, when the eternal new year will be inaugurated. Then our shouts will bring about the fall of Jericho's walls of wickedness and will proclaim to those who stand beside the Ark of the Covenant the Lord's eternal enthronement.

There are, therefore, feasts that have not been completely suppressed but that are held, as it were, in abeyance until their new and completely spiritualized object has been definitively realized. The Jewish feast is a basic element in the formulation of Christian eschatology.

7 The trumpet that will be heard on the first day of eternity is better known as "the trumpet of the last judgment." But this association of the trumpet with the judgment may have had its origin in the ancient context of the new year. In fact we have seen that on the pagan new year, lots were drawn to learn the god's judgment that would determine the destiny of the world and men during the coming year. The present Jewish New Year service includes prayers in which the theme of judgment frequently recurs. (Cf. *Rosh ha Schana,* the book of prayers, ed. Durlacher). Perhaps the theme of judgment was introduced or at least developed in a new-year context.

Chapter Four

the Feast of Harvests or Feast of Tents

A. PRELIMINARIES

The feasts which belonged to what we have called the rhythm of astronomy have not been introduced into the Christian calendar although they were adopted by and given a spiritual meaning in the Jewish religion. Because of its eschatological symbolism, one of these feasts, that of a New Year, was not completely rejected by the New Testament; yet it, too, is missing in the new liturgy.

We shall now examine three agrarian feasts: the feast of Harvest in the seventh month and the two feasts of offering of sheaves in the first and third months. Here the results will be more positive since two of these feasts have been inscribed in the Christian calendar, but only after a process of spiritualization.

It is these laws of spiritualization that we shall try to determine. How can a merely human feast become a Christian feast? If astronomical feasts have found no place in the calendars of men freed from the rhythm of creation, how can feasts based on agrarian work deserve to be included in a Christian calendar? Why should an agrarian feast like the feast of Harvests be rejected while two similar feasts were accepted?

Perhaps when we have clarified these laws, we will be able to show some of the lessons that a catechesis of our feasts and rites should include, so that their specifically Christian content will be plain. No doubt we will also be able to determine the kind of culture, agrarian or nomadic, worker or middle class, etc., that the feast represents and why. Lastly, we will be able to understand how human rites can eventually be transposed to the Christian plane and we can list a whole series of tasks they must pass if they are to deserve this consecration.

B. FROM THE AGRARIAN TO THE NOMADIC

When the Jews settled in Canaan they found that feasts at the time of the harvests of fruits and the gathering of grapes were celebrated throughout the land. Long before their arrival the natives had adopted a form of sedentary and agrarian life while the Jews were still, practically speaking, in the nomadic stage. We possess two descriptions of the feast of the Harvest as it was observed shortly after the Jewish invasion. It seems, at least in the first case, that these feasts were reserved to the Canaanites and that the Jews had not yet begun to celebrate them. This is understandable if the feasts were agrarian in origin and the Jews had not yet reached that cultural level. It is significant that they took advantage of these Canaanite festivals to attack the merry-making crowds. This indicates that they found these feasts strange, probably because they could not recognize in them their own desert spirituality. But let the texts speak for themselves:

> The citizens of Sichem [Canaanite notables] then set men in ambush for him [Abimelech] on the mountain-tops, and these robbed all who passed them on the road. But it was reported to Abimelech. Now Gaal, son of Obed, came over to Sichem with his kinsmen. The citizens of Sichem put their trust in him, and went out into the fields, harvested their grapes and trod them out. Then they held a festival and went to the temple of their god, where they ate and drank and cursed Abimelech. . . . The next day when the people were taking the field, it was reported to Abimelech, who divided the men he had into three companies, and set up an ambush in the fields. He watched till he saw the people leave the city and then rose against them for the attack. . . . So he went up Mount Selmon with all his soldiers, took his ax in his hand, and cut down some brushwood. This he lifted to his shoulder, then said to the men with him, "Hurry! Do just as you have seen me do." So all the men likewise cut down brushwood, and following Abimelech, placed it against the crypt. Then they set the crypt on fire over their heads, so that every one of the citizens of Magdal-Sichem [where the Canaanite notables had hidden], about a thousand men and women, perished (Judg. 9:25-49).

This text needs no long commentary. The Sichemites were busy harvesting their vines and were combining pleasure with work. Allusion is made to most of the elements of the pagan harvest feast: rejoicing, sacred banquets, living in the open fields, but there is no mention of the temporary huts that were usually constructed on these occasions. Even the branches cut from trees and which were probably waved during the festive gathering were parodied by King Abimelech to the ruin of his enemies. This episode leaves us with the impression that the Jews had not yet adopted this feast since they seized this opportunity to attack those who were taking part and, as part of their strategy, mimicked one of the essential rites.

The second passage from the book of Judges is equally explicit. The Benjaminites had just been defeated by the other tribes because they had isolated themselves from the confederation. As a result their daughters were captured or killed and the tribes vowed never to allow their own girls to marry Benjaminite men. This is the way the Benjaminites secured wives for themselves outside the confederation:

> Then they [the members of the other tribes] thought of the yearly feast of the Lord at Silo, north of Bethel, east of the highway that goes up from Bethel to Sichem, and south of Lebona. And they instructed the Benjaminites, "Go and lie in wait in the vineyards. When you see the girls of Silo come out to do their dancing, leave the vineyards and each of you seize one of the girls of Silo for a wife, and go to the land of Benjamin. . . . The Benjaminites did this; they carried off a wife for each of them from their raid on the

> dancers, and went back to their own territory, where they rebuilt and occupied the cities (Judg. 21: 19-23).

The Benjaminites used the same tactics that had succeeded at Sichem. They took advantage of a feast celebrated by the pagan people of Silo (the reference to the vines suggests that it was the feast of the grape harvest) and of a special rite of this feast (the dance of the young girls), to rush in when their enemies were no doubt too much influenced by excessive eating and drinking to be able to react immediately. We may suppose that all the Jews had not adopted this agrarian feast which did not accord with their nomadic culture.[8]

The Israelites were not slow to add this feast to their calendar. They probably did this as soon as they had driven away the original inhabitants and had begun to cultivate their land. Two of the oldest legislative texts include this feast in the Jewish calendar. As in pagan times it was observed during the seventh month.

> Three times a year you shall celebrate a pilgrim feast to me. You shall keep the feast of Unleavened Bread. . . . You shall also keep the feast of the grain harvest . . . and finally, the feast at the fruit harvest at the end of year, when you gather in the produce from the fields (Ex. 23:14-16).

At that time our September was the first month of the year, so this feast was placed at the end of the preceding month or during the first days of this month. Later texts will be more exact about the date and the feast will de-

8 No doubt the old tradition recorded in this passage was later modified to agree with the history of the Ark at Silo. Thus the pagan feast was referred to as "a feast of Yahweh."

finitely be assigned to the fifteenth day of the seventh month.

An old Yahwist text refers to this feast under its ancient pagan and agrarian name of "the feast of the Harvest":

> You shall keep the feast of Weeks with the first of the wheat harvest; likewise, the feast at the fruit harvest at the close of the year (Ex. 34:22).

Does this mean that the Hebrews had accepted all the agrarian elements of the feast? Possibly they did so in the beginning. Soon there was a reaction. The feast was given a nomadic dimension as is clear in Deuteronomy.

The pagan custom of living in temporary huts when the vines were being dressed was originally no more than a time-saving device. No mention is made of this practice either at Sichem or Silo in the two texts cited above. Perhaps it had not yet become general or its purpose was so functional that it was scarcely worth recording. Yet it was these huts that were to serve as the point of departure for the spiritualization of this feast. In Deuteronomy they were made the symbol of the tents in which the people lived during their nomadic days in the desert. So important did this symbol become that the feast lost its old agrarian name and was known as "the feast of Huts," "feast of Tents," or "feast of Booths":

> You shall celebrate the feast of booths for seven days, when you have gathered in the produce from your threshing floor and wine press. You shall make merry at your feast, together with your son and daughter, your male and female slave, and also the Levite, the alien, the orphan and the

> widow who belong to your community. For seven days you shall celebrate this pilgrim feast in honor of the Lord, your God, in the place which he chooses; since the Lord, your God, has blessed you in all your crops and in all your undertakings, you shall do naught but make merry. Three times a year, then, every male among you shall appear before the Lord, your God, in the place which he chooses: at the feast of Unleavened Bread, at the feast of Weeks, and at the feast of Booths (Deut. 16:13-16).

Notice that this text is wholly orientated towards the old agrarian feast: products of threshing floor and wine press, general merry-making, etc. Only the name of the feast is new.

The explanation of this change is found in an addition made to the Levitical calendar.

> By perpetual statute for you and your descendants you shall keep this pilgrim feast of the Lord for one whole week in the seventh month of the year. During this week every native Israelite among you shall dwell in booths, that your descendants may realize that, when I led the Israelites out of the land of Egypt, I made them dwell in booths. I, the Lord, am your God" (Lev. 23:41-43).

When discussing the feasts of the pagan world, we described the fusion of nomadic and agrarian feasts. In the Jewish world, on the contrary, there is strictly speaking no fusion, but rather a transformation of an agrarian rite into a nomadic rite. We shall have the opportunity to note other modifications of this kind which were obviously intentional. We may even go so far as to say that no rite, agrarian in origin, preserved its agrarian significance in the Jewish world. This means that the Jewish liturgy (and this will also be true later of the Christian liturgy) did not necessarily adopt the rites of any culture at all. It would be foolish to hope that every civilization and every culture could be introduced into the liturgy. Yet there is one culture which has been singularly favored above all others: this is the nomadic culture because it recalls the years in the desert and is a sign of the paschal state of God's people marching towards the Kingdom. The liturgy does not gather together men comfortably settled in their own lands, but men who are nomads, who are always becoming, always looking forward, always dissatisfied with conditions such as they find them here below. And if some rites derived from other cultures, such as the agrarian culture, have persisted in the Jewish and later in the Christian liturgy, it is not because of their original significance but because of the nomadic characteristics which have been superimposed upon them.

The first form of the spiritualization of the harvest, therefore, consists in its transposition from the agrarian to the nomadic plane. There is also a second and concurrent transposition which we shall now examine.

C. FROM NATURE TO HISTORY

The spiritualization realized by the deuteronomist movement has another significance which will be far-reaching in the final evolution of the liturgy. Selecting among the different rites of the harvest feast those of paramount interest for its own purpose, this movement added to them a new historical significance:

> During this week every native Israelite among you shall dwell in booths, that your descendants may realize that, when I led the Israelites out of the land of Egypt, I made them dwell in booths. I, the Lord, am your God (Lev. 23:43).

In this way for the first time in the history of the Jewish liturgy, a rite originally derived from nature lost its original meaning and was made the expression of an historic event. The feast no longer symbolized the rhythm of nature but the development of history guided by the hand of God. For the first time a rite recalled not only an annual natural occurrence but a free and gratuitous act of God. Henceforth it is not the rhythm of creation that will impose its law on rites and liturgical feasts, but God's will and His intervention in the world. This spiritualization is important because it also transforms the essence of worship itself, which is not primarily a religious act of man on the occasion of a natural event but the representation, as it were, of an act of God that man recalls and in some way renews. As a result of this passage to the historic plane (and of this we shall soon have other examples), God is given primacy in the feast because it is recognized that He directs history, and the Hebrew who takes part in this feast benefits in his turn from the historic action.

This reference to the years in the desert resulted in a gradual elimination of all agrarian elements of the feast and the substitution of a new commemorative element. One of the consequences of this spiritualization, the rite of the renewal of the desert covenant, became important. Since the people dwelt in huts to recall the stay in the desert, was it not essential that they renew their covenant with God and promise the fidelity that they had so often compromised? This is precisely the point stressed in those texts of Deuteronomy that are responsible for the spiritualization of this feast and that are the best source of information for the renewal of the covenant.

> When Moses had written down this law, he entrusted it to the Levitical priests who carry the Ark of the Covenant of the Lord, and to all the elders of Israel, giving them this order: "On the feast of Booths, at the prescribed time in the year of relaxation which comes at the end of every seven-year period, when all Israel goes to appear before the Lord, your God, in the place which he chooses, you shall read this law aloud in the presence of all Israel. Assemble the people—men, women and children, as well as the aliens who live in your communities—that they may hear it and learn it, and so fear the Lord, your God, and carefully observe all the words of this law. Their children also, who do not know it yet, must hear it and learn it, that they too may fear the Lord, your God, as long as you live on the land which you will cross the Jordan to occupy (Deut. 31:9-13).

Moreover, it is possible that Deuteronomy may even provide us with the liturgical text of the proclamation of the law, in the form of a litany in which the people repeat their ratification by a kind of refrain after each article:

> 'Cursed be the man who makes a carved or molten idol—an abomination to the Lord, the product of a craftsman's hands—and sets it up in secret!' And all the people shall answer, 'Amen!'
> 'Cursed be he who dishonors his father or his mother!' And all the people shall answer, 'Amen!'

> 'Cursed be he who moves his neighbor's landmarks!' And all the people shall answer, 'Amen!'
> 'Cursed be he who misleads a blind man on his way!' And all the people shall answer, 'Amen!'
> 'Cursed be he who violates the rights of the alien, the orphan or the widow!' And all the people shall answer, 'Amen!'
> 'Cursed be he who has relations with his father's wife, for he dishonors his father's bed!' And all the people shall answer, 'Amen!'
> 'Cursed be he who has relations with any animal!' And all the people shall answer, 'Amen!'
> 'Cursed be he who has relations with his sister or his half-sister!' And all the people shall answer, 'Amen!'
> 'Cursed be he who has relations with his mother-in-law!' And all the people shall answer, 'Amen!'
> 'Cursed be he who slays his neighbor in secret!' And all the people shall answer, 'Amen!'
> 'Cursed be he who accepts payment for slaying an innocent man!' And all the people shall answer, 'Amen!'
> 'Cursed be he who fails to fulfill any of the provisions of this law!' And all the people shall answer, 'Amen!' (Deut. 27:15-26).

Later, as a result of the development of the feast of Pentecost, the theme of the renewal of the law will be moved to that feast so that it, too, will possess what it had hitherto lacked, a reference to the stay in the desert. This will be discussed below.[9]

Libations of water provide us with another example of the transition from the plane of nature to that of history, as we learn from the Jewish legends connected with the rite of the seventh month. We have shown that these libations were probably part of an old pagan ceremony in which the gift of rain was implored so that the land

[9] Cf. p. 143 ff.

might be fertile. To ensure a prosperous year, water was drawn from a fountain and poured in copious streams on the ground. This was an agrarian rite that the Hebrews seem to have adopted without making any change. But in the course of time it was transformed. The *Sukka* (Tents) treatise in the Talmud has abundant details on this subject. In procession water was carried from Silo to the temple, then poured on the altar and on the ground while prayers were recited asking for a fruitful year. Now the bare rock of Mount Sion was visible in the temple ground and a legend soon explained that this was the rock that had accompanied the people during their desert trek and supplied them regularly with living water. A surprising echo of this legend is found in St. Paul:

> And all ate the same spiritual food, and drank the same spiritual drink (for they drank from the spiritual rock which followed them, and the rock was Christ) (1 Cor. 10:4).

While water was being poured on the temple ground it was customary to read the account of the miracle of the rock of living water; in this way the historic fact was superimposed on the natural significance of fertility and the nomadic experience eclipsed the agrarian rite. Following this clue, many exegetes have wanted to find a spiritualization of the same kind in such secondary themes as the cloud, the mountain, etc.[10]

It would be dangerous to go too far in our interpretation of these minor details. Here let it suffice to observe that the Jews did not syncretize pagan feasts introduced

10 See Riesenfeld, *Le Christ transfiguré*.

into their worship but, on the contrary, they introduced into these feasts their own experience of God in the desert-event.

D. FROM HISTORY TO ESCHATOLOGY

The memory of all that had happened in the desert began to fade with the passage of the years. As these events became more and more remote they seemed no longer relevant or even helpful in the catastrophic situation in which the people found themselves, weakened by sin or persecution. There then arose a prophetic movement that sought to give new interest to these old desert experiences by projecting them to a not too-distant eschatological future. Feasts that had up until then commemorated striking incidents in the desert would henceforth signify, in addition to the memory of the past, the expectation of similar experiences in the future; that would lead to a liberation more total and more perfect than the old liberation had been. It is, therefore, not surprising that the rites of the feast of the seventh month were re-thought in terms of the new eschatological situation. Thus the feast became, as it were, a general rehearsal through its rites, of what would one day mark the inauguration of the messianic era. This will be plain if we examine what post-exilic authors have to say about the symbolism of each of these rites.

The rite of the *water libation,* as we have seen, had its origin in an agrarian context. Perhaps this rite once was part of an autumn feast in honor of the first rain and later it was combined with the feast of Tents. But this rite then developed in a context of the stay in the desert and recalled this stay in its own way. Now the Deutero-Isaias announced a new sojourn in the desert in which fountains of living water would flow in the steppe, gladdening the people during their journey.

> I will open up rivers on the bare heights, and fountains in the broad valleys; I will turn the desert into a marshland, and the dry grounds into springs of water.
> I will plant in the desert the cedar, acacia, myrtle, and olive; I will set in the wasteland the cypress, together with the plane tree and the pine (Is. 41:18-19).[11]

Thus it is not surprising that Hebrew commentators saw in the libation rite, not merely the ancient water-giving rock but the promise of the living waters that would flow in the messianic era. Ezechiel takes the first step. Zacharias follows him closely. Ezechiel's vision of the messianic era, with its comment on the libation of water and the feast of Tents, is significant.

> Then he [the angel] brought me back to the entrance of the temple, and I saw water flowing out from beneath the threshold of the temple toward the east, for the facade of the temple was toward the east; the water flowed down from the southern side of the temple, south of the altar. He led me outside by the north gate, and around to the outer gate facing the east, where I saw water trickling from the southern side. Then when he had walked off to the east with a measuring cord in his hand, he measured off a

11 Note that the tree theme, as well as the theme of desert water, is important in the feast of Tents. Later we shall point out its eschatological significance.

> thousand cubits and had me wade through the water, which was ankle-deep. He measured off another thousand and once more had me wade through the water, which was now knee-deep. Again he measured off a thousand and had me wade; the water was up to my waist. Once more he measured off a thousand, but there was now a river through which I could not wade; for the water had risen so high it had become a river that could not be crossed except by swimming. He asked me, "Have you seen this, son of man?" Then he brought me to the bank of the river, where he had me sit. Along the bank of the river I saw very many trees on both sides. He said to me, "This water flows into the eastern district down upon the Araba, and empties into the sea, the salt waters, which it makes fresh. Wherever the river flows, every sort of living creature that can multiply shall live, and there shall be abundant fish, for wherever this water comes the sea shall be made fresh. Fishermen shall be standing along it from En-gaddi to En-gallim, spreading their nets there. Its kinds of fish shall be like those of the Great Sea, very numerous (Ez. 47:1-10).

Thus the minor rite of pouring water on the altar was the beginning of a river of paradise that was to bring life wherever it passed and was able to purify the water of the sea. This river carried with it an extraordinary abundance of fish (this the Apostles were to verify in the miraculous catch) and was to give birth to many trees of life. It might be claimed that the agrarian theme is still basic in this description, but it is evident that, even in Ezechiel's eyes, the agrarian fertility theme is but a symbol. It has become the sign of a deeper reality, that of the new economy in which the Spirit of God will shower in abundance the water of His grace.

> This is the meditation of the Second Zacharias on the same subject: On that day there shall no longer be cold or frost. There shall be one continuous day, known to the Lord, not

day and night, for in the evening time there shall be light. On that day, living waters shall flow from Jerusalem, half to the eastern sea, and half to the western sea, and it shall be so in summer and in winter. The Lord shall become king over the whole earth; on that day the Lord shall be the only one, and his name the only one. And from Geba to Rimmon in the Negeb, all the land shall turn into a plain; but Jerusalem shall remain exalted in its place. From the Gate of Benjamin to the place of the First Gate, to the Corner Gate; and from the Tower of Hananeel to the king's wine presses, they shall occupy her. Never again shall she be doomed; Jerusalem shall abide in security. And this shall be the plague with which the Lord shall strike all the nations that have fought against Jerusalem: their flesh shall rot while they stand upon their feet, and their eyes shall rot in their sockets, and their tongues shall rot in their mouths. On that day there shall be among them a great tumult from the Lord: every man shall seize the hand of his neighbor, and the hand of each shall be raised against that of his neighbor. Juda also shall fight against Jerusalem. The riches of all the surrounding nations shall be gathered together, gold, silver, and garments, in great abundance. Similar to this plague shall be the plague upon the horses, mules, camels, asses, and upon all the beasts that are in those camps. All who are left of all the nations that came against Jerusalem shall come up year after year to worship the King, the Lord of hosts, and to celebrate the feast of Tabernacles (Zach. 14: 6-16).

If Zacharias repeats the theme of Ezechiel's meditation, he explains the symbolism more clearly when he associates the living water with universal recognition of Yahweh's kingship. The feast of the seventh month, like the feast of the New Year, since pagan days, had been a feast of the enthronement of a god. Now the living water, showered upon all the nations in the form of graces, will ensure the kingship of Yahweh who is enthroned over the whole universe. This theme of eschatological water had special meaning for the Jewish people, who knew so well the sterility of the Dead Sea in whose waters no fish could survive. According to the biblical account, it was the sin of Sodom and Gomorrah that was responsible for this sterility. It would be the gift of water poured down on Jerusalem that would assure increase of life. Thus the water rite continued to signify "fertility," just as it once did on the human level but this fertility was now none other than the life God Himself communicates to man in the later days.

The rite of new fruits and branches underwent the same eschatological re-reading. We saw Abimelech's sacrilegious parody of the rite of branches in the massacre of Sichemite notables (Judg. 9), but as soon as the Jewish people adopted the feast of the seventh month, the cutting down of branches and their use in procession became an important element of the liturgy:

> And they kept eight days with joy, after the manner of the feast of the Tabernacles. . . . Therefore they now carried boughs and green branches and palms for him that had given them good success in cleansing his place (2 Mach. 10:6-7).

Like all the other rites of this feast, this one was spiritualized on the historic plane when the branches thus cut down were used to construct huts to recall the stay in the desert:

> And they found written in the law, that the Lord had commanded by the hand of Moses, that the children of Israel should dwell in tabernacles, on the feast, in the seventh

> month. And that they should proclaim and publish the word in all their cities, and in Jerusalem, saying: Go forth to the mount, and fetch branches of olive, and branches of beautiful wood, branches of myrtle, and branches of palm, and branches of thick trees, to make tabernacles, as it is written (Neh. 8:14-15).

The eschatological and paradisal aspect is the final significance attached to this rite. We have seen that Ezechiel described the trees of life planted on the banks of the river of living waters. The prophet had gone further and announced that the desert itself, thanks to the living water, would produce all kinds of fruit trees:

> Along both banks of the river, fruit trees of every kind shall grow; their leaves shall not fade, nor their fruit fail. Every month they shall bear fresh fruit, for they shall be watered by the flow from the sanctuary. Their fruit shall serve for food, and their leaves for medicine (Ez. 47:12).

Thus the merrymaking of the harvest of fruits and the gathering of grapes signified the joy of the coming heavenly era. In biblical literature, harvest and vintage were used henceforth to denote apocalyptic realities that will prelude the end of time.

Even the *rite of tents* acquired an eschatological meaning. The prophet had foretold that some day there would be another sojourn in the desert. Once again the people would live in tents grouped about the tent of reunion as part of their preparation to enter the new promised land:

> I am the Lord, your God, since the land of Egypt; I will again have you live in tents, as in that appointed time. I granted many visions and spoke to the prophets, through whom I set forth examples (Osee 12:9-10).

These tents will be signs of eschatological happiness:

> Then will the desert become an orchard and the orchard be regarded as a forest. Right will dwell in the desert and justice abide in the orchard. Justice will bring about peace; right will produce calm and security. My people will live in peaceful country, in secure dwellings and quiet resting places (Is. 32:15-18).

Judaism developed this theme and we find many refences to it in the New Testament. The just, who form but a small remnant in these eschatological days, will live in tents. The messiah himself will dwell in their midst in a magnificent tent, a replica of the tent of Yahweh which was always in the center of the camp the Jews pitched in the Sinai desert (Jn. 1:14).

The rite of the *royal enthronement* also acquired eschatological spiritualization. It was especially at a time when no king sat upon the throne in Juda or Israel that this rite was further spiritualized. Psalm 117, messianic in inspiration, was composed for one of the processions of the feast of the seventh month.

> The joyful shout of victory in the tents of the just. . . . Blessed is he who comes in the name of the Lord: we bless you from the house of the Lord. The Lord is God, and he has given us light. Join in procession with leafy boughs up to the horns of the altar (Ps. 117:15-27).

Notice how the different elements of the feast of the New Year and the feast of Tents are fused together: the "shouters," the "tents," the "palms," and, crowning all, the appeal to Him who comes.

If we were to turn from our study of scriptural texts to a study of the Jewish ritual, we could easily find many more supporting texts. Yet they would be of only secondary interest. Furthermore, we would have to be sure that the ritual is earlier than the New Testament.[12] But additional evidence is not necessary because our purpose is not to be exhaustive; rather it is to discover the thread that links the human rite with its fulfillment in the Christian liturgy. We are now in a position to say that the rites of the feast were spiritualized first by investing them with the historic experience of the people when they were in the desert,[13] then with a new prophetic and eschatological meaning belonging to the messianic era. Thus the feast of Tents continued to be celebrated and became a preparation for the events that were to come, an alerting of the people summoned to the happiness of the end-time.[14]

E. THE FEAST FINDS ITS REAL OBJECT IN CHRIST

The Gospels record two rather unusual incidents which, in their original form in the primitive catechesis, had for their setting Christ's participation in the feasts of the seventh month. Later editing, for reasons which we will explain, suppressed all explicit allusions to the feast of

12 Snaith, *The Jewish New Year Festival,* London, 1948, is fairly skeptical on this subject.

13 Cf. Kraus, *Gottesdienst im Israël,* Munich, 1954.

14 Read with certain reservations Daniélou, *Symbolisme eschatologique des Tabernacles,* Irenikon, 1958, pp. 19 ff.

Tents but preserved the other details of these incidents for their own sake.

The first incident is the Transfiguration, which seems to have been composed in such a way that contemporaries saw in it the description of the ritual of the feast of Tents fulfilled in the person of Christ Himself. Sound reasons indicate that the ritual described was not that of Jerusalem but of Galilee.[15] Notice some of the characteristics of this feast:

> Then Peter addressed Jesus, saying, "Lord, it is good for us to be here. If thou wilt, let us set up three tents here, one for thee, one for Moses, and one for Elias" (Mt. 17:4).

When Peter saw Christ transfigured, he apparently recalled that the messiah would dwell in a tent surrounded by the just during the last days:

> As he was still speaking, behold, a bright cloud overshadowed them, and behold, a voice out of the cloud said, "This is my beloved Son, in whom I am well pleased: hear Him" (Mt. 17:5).

In this sentence we may find the messianic enthronement formula of the new-year rite. "Well beloved son" of God there denoted the messiah-king. Furthermore, the themes of mountain and cloud, briefly mentioned in our analysis of the feast of Tents, were important parts of the feast and prominent in Judaism.

The Lord's desire to be transfigured before the Apostles in the very special setting of the autumn feast suggests that He was presenting Himself as the object of the feast.

15 See Riesenfeld, *The Transfiguration.*

The second text is even more explicit. Many elements in this description of Christ's entrance into Jerusalem (Mt. 21), can be explained only in the context of the feast of the seventh month. Ignoring for a moment the fact that this going up to Jerusalem is actually presented in a paschal context, let us only examine its internal changes.

There is, first, the statement that the cortege accompanying the Lord is singing psalm 119, the traditional psalm for this feast, as its title indicates:

> And the crowds that went before him, and those that followed, kept crying out, saying, "Hosanna to the Son of David! Blessed is he who comes in the name of the Lord!" (Mt. 21:9).

When Luke explicitly refers to the "acclamation" which accompanied the psalm, he seems to wish to recall the acclamations of the new-year feast connected with the feast of Tents (Lk. 19:37). To escort Him whom they believed to be the long-expected messiah, the Jews cut branches:

> And most of the crowd spread their cloaks upon the road, while others were cutting branches from the trees, and strewing them on the road (Mt. 21:8).

This is plainly the gesture prescribed by the Law for the feast of Tents and it is difficult to believe that it could have taken place during the first month of the year when the leaves have just appeared and the trees are more respected.

This theme of new fruits and branches is referred to a little later when Christ, standing before a fig tree, wishes to gather its fruit but finds nothing but leaves:

> Now in the morning, on his way back to the city, he felt hungry. And seeing a fig tree by the wayside, he came up to it, and found nothing on it but leaves; and he said to it, "May no fruit ever come from thee henceforth forever!" And immediately the fig tree withered up (Mt. 21:18-19).

If this episode occurred, as it does according to the present Gospel tradition, in a paschal context (that is, during the first month), Christ's action is absolutely incomprehensible because He must have known that fig trees bear no fruit during the first month. Mark, indeed, believes that he has solved this difficulty by asserting:

> for it was not the season for figs (Mk. 11:13).

In reality this episode can only be understood if it is placed in its original setting: a feast of Tents, during the seventh month, when the harvest of fruits is celebrated and when fig trees are expected to be covered with fruit. On that occasion Christ's action would have manifested His concern over the failure of the Jewish dispensation to bear the fruit God expected. The inadequacy of the feast of Tents was now clear: the feast of the agrarian harvest, the feast of the eschatological harvest, should also have been the feast of the harvest of fruits of submission to the Law and fidelity to the Covenant instead of fruits of lies and hypocrisy. The progressive spiritualizations realized in the Old Testament were not accompanied by the moral advances that alone would have guaranteed the continued existence of the feast, but whose absence revealed its ephemeral nature.

Another episode, also related by the Synoptics within the frame of reference of the entry into Jerusalem, acquires new meaning if we wish to see in it the counterpart of the rites of the feast of Tabernacles. This is the expulsion of the sellers from the temple.

These men played an important role in the observance of the feast of Tents. For several centuries the Jews had not carried the produce of their fields and flocks to Jerusalem. The hazards of travel made the fulfillment of these obligations too difficult. So it became the custom to sell at home what they intended to offer in the temple. Carrying this sum to Jerusalem (a very simple matter), they exchanged it there for the fruit or cattle they wished to offer in sacrifice. The temple merchants made this exchange possible. Zacharias, in his important description of the eschatological feast of Tents, insists that in those later days of superabundance, everything will be procured without cost and that the poor themselves will be able to secure as much as they want to offer to God:

> And every caldron in Jerusalem and Juda shall be sanctified to the Lord of hosts: and all that sacrifice shall come, and take of them and shall seethe in them: and the merchant shall be no more in the house of the Lord of hosts in that day (Zach. 14:21).

So when Christ drove the sellers from the temple, He wished to fulfill the prophecy of Zacharias and to show

how He Himself was the fulfillment of the eschatological feast of Tents foretold by the prophets.

Moreover, it is not impossible that Christ also wished to realize an aspect of the feast of Tents which we have not yet analyzed in detail: the rite of expiation. This rite goes back to pagan times when temples were completely purified at the new year of all the preceding year's defilements. Was Christ not seeking an expiation and a purification of another order when He drove the sellers out of the temple, so that His Father's house might become once more a house of prayer? Was His action not a way of saying that another new year, a new dispensation, was now beginning which would require the rejection of all that had been done heretofore?

Christ's entry into Jerusalem and its accompanying episodes acquire a fullness of meaning when considered in the context of the feast of the seventh month: the true feast of Tents, expected in the last days, now finds its center in the person of Christ. The last days have already begun, the feast has attained its real object.

But at this moment the feast shatters into fragments: the episode of the cursed fig tree, the sellers expelled from the temple, the arrival of a poor messiah, seated on an ass when he was expected in power and glory—all these incidents, without precedent in Jewish ritual, point to its failure. The feast disappears when it attains its object. The harvest of fruit it celebrated was a harvest of bad fruit, and the introduction of temple-sellers led to formalism. The right attitude of soul was no part of the feast.

Strangled by formalism, it disappeared at the very summit of its development.

F. THE FEAST BECOMES A PERSON

The two synoptic accounts that we have just analyzed made Jesus the object of the feast of Tents. John, reflecting on this much later, saw that Jesus was not only the object of the feast but the feast itself. So, if the feast is abolished, it is because it is to continue in the person of Jesus Himself.

We can witness this personification in an account describing Christ's participation in a feast of Tents:

> Now on the last, the great day of the feast, Jesus stood and cried out, saying, "If anyone thirst, let him come to me and drink. He who believes in me, as the Scripture says, 'From within him there shall flow rivers of living water' " (Jn. 7:37-38).

On the last day of the feast a procession was formed to bring water from the fountain of Silo to the temple, where it was poured on the altar and the rock, in memory of the rock of living water. No doubt it was during this procession that Christ presented Himself as the new rock of living water from which would flow rivers of living water. Christ thus drew into His own person what hitherto had been contained in the libation rite. He is not only the object of the feast but He Himself is the rite.

It will be recalled that Christ had already said to the Samaritan woman:

> "If thou didst know the gift of God, and who it is who says to thee, 'Give me to drink,' thou, perhaps wouldst have asked of him, and he would have given thee living water. . . . Everyone who drinks of this water will thirst again. He, however, who drinks of the water that I will give him shall never thirst; but the water that I will give him shall become in him a fountain of water, springing up into life everlasting" (Jn. 4:10-14).

This means that the feast has been transcended in Christ. No need for us to offer libations of water when we possess in our midst One who is the unfailing source of living water.

Certain rites of this feast had been personified in the Old Testament: for example, the expiation that had once been connected with the feast of the seventh month. We have seen that at Sumer the temple was purified on that occasion by the body of a lamb. This rite was elaborated in the Jewish priestly legislation concerning the two scapegoats (Lev. 16; 23:26-32; Num. 29:7-11). While the priests were busy formulating this ritual, Trito-Isaias had begun to personalize it by describing it in human terms—the Suffering Servant who took upon himself all the world's sin and suffering:

> Surely he hath borne our infirmities and carried our sorrows: and we have thought him as it were a leper, and as one struck by God and afflicted. But he was wounded for our iniquities: he was bruised for our sins. The chastisement of our peace was upon him: and by his bruises we are healed (Is. 53:4-5).

Thus we see the appearance of a new test in the spiritualization of a rite or feast: the power of signifying the person of Christ. In fact, the feast of Tents was never fully capable of bearing the mystery of the person of Christ and that is why it disappeared or was at least absorbed into other feasts.

G. THE FEAST OF TENTS BECOMES THE FEAST OF EASTER

We shall see in this section devoted to the historic evolution of the paschal feast that even in the Old Testament so great an effort was made to endow this feast with some of the privileges of the feast of Tents, that it was deprived of the privilege of being a new-year feast and lost its position of pre-eminence.

Primitive Christian tradition seems to have wished to continue this trend when Christ's entry into Jerusalem was moved from the seventh month to the first month so that it might be given a paschal context.[16]

This perspective corresponds with the way certain Old Testament texts are handled in the New. References to reaping, grape-gathering and harvesting abound in the Old Testament. The Hebrew was too attached to the earth not to care about the fruits of his work and when the prophets began to speak about the end of time, they often made use of these themes. In this climate of thought, the feast of Harvests could continue and develop. Now the Gospel, and especially Christ, rarely speak of harvests

16 Daniélou, "Les Quatre-Temps de septembre et la fête des Tabernacles," *La Maison-Dieu*, 46, pp. 114-136. Let us note, incidentally, that the author shows how the Ember Days still retain allusions to the old feast of Tents.

and direct the reader's attention to a theme unknown in the Old Testament: that of seeds and sowing. It is easy to see why our Lord preferred this theme: before the time to reap and harvest, must come the slow and mysterious work of the seed that dies in the earth in order to bear fruit, that grows in the midst of weeds and is always in danger of being choked, that falls on all kinds of soil and is often unable to take root and grow. Harvesting denotes richness, fertility, power; sowing denotes poverty (the mustard seed), death, disappointment. . . .

A harvest there will indeed be, but it will be preceded by death and the slow, difficult transformation of the seed. This is not to deny eschatology, but it is to show that this eschatology comes only after long centuries during which the Church, slowly and patiently, in painful childbirth, will prepare for what was begun in the death of Christ.

This explains why the most important characteristics of the paschal feast became, on the Christian plane, the feast of the seed that dies in the earth to newness of life. That is why John insists that the true rock of living water was revealed when the centurion struck the side of Christ and there poured forth a life-giving stream:

> But one of the soldiers opened his side with a lance, and immediately there came out blood and water (Jn. 19:34).

This is the same transposition of the enthronement rite to the entrance into Jerusalem, which was moved from the seventh month to the first (Mt. 21). Christ's words to

His Apostles after the transfiguration (which was a way of celebrating the feast of Tents) reveal the same desire to connect this incident henceforth with the paschal mystery.

> "Tell the vision to no one, till the Son of Man has risen from the dead" (Mt. 17:9).

The rite of expiation is another example of transposition. As soon as Isaias, as we have seen, personalized the rite of expiation in the person of the Suffering Servant, he made it possible to understand the feast of expiation in paschal terms.

Our final transposition remains. The Apocalypse sees in the paschal cross the tree of life foretold in the context of the feast of Tents:

> Him who overcomes I will permit to eat of the tree of life, which is in the paradise of my God (Apoc. 2:7).

In the primitive Church, therefore, certain elements of the feast of Tents were modified and added to the feast of Easter. This does not mean that life's eschatological dimension was relegated to second place but merely that it cannot be perfectly expressed without reference to the conditions on which it is acquired, namely the death, the resurrection, and the slow growth of the seed. This is why the feast of Tents lost its position of primacy in the liturgical year and no longer inaugurated the new year. In the primitive catechesis, notes once reserved for the feast of Tents were transferred to Easter. Had there been only the incarnation, the feast of Tents could have sufficed: Christ, in His own person, sufficiently fulfilled its symbols. But the incarnation cannot be separated from the redemption. So these symbols cannot adequately denote Christ unless they are able to express the mystery of the Cross. Christian tradition realized this and made Easter the first feast. To understand the mystery of Christ, is to understand the Cross and the Resurrection.

H. THERE WILL BE ANOTHER FEAST OF TENTS

While this adjustment was being made, the Apocalypse described the future celebration of a new feast of Tents:

> After this I saw a great multitude which no man could number, out of all nations and tribes and peoples and tongues, standing before the throne and before the Lamb, clothed in white robes, and with palms in their hands. And they cried with a loud voice, saying, "Salvation belongs to our God who sits upon the throne, and to the Lamb. . . . And one of the elders spoke and said to me, "These who are clothed in white robes, who are they? and whence have they come?" And I said to him, "My lord, thou knowest." And he said to me, "These are they who have come out of the great tribulation, and have washed their robes and made them white in the blood of the lamb. Therefore, they are before the throne of God, and serve him day and night in his temple, and he who sits upon the throne will dwell with them. . . . For the Lamb who is in the midst of the throne will shepherd them, and will guide them to the fountains of the waters of life, and God will wipe away every tear from their eyes" (Apoc. 7:9-17).

This is a description of the celebration of a feast of Tents at the dawn of the eschatological days. This is the long procession of every nation and every race foreseen by Zacharias for the feast of Tents:

> And all they that shall be left of all nations . . . shall go up from year to year to adore the King, the Lord of hosts, and to keep the feast of tabernacles (Zach 14:16).

The sumptuous tent reserved for the messiah will shelter all the just who will eternally share with him his messianic gifts: "He who sits upon the throne will dwell with them." There is also a reference to the rite of shouting: the "mighty voice" with which the elect hymned "salvation to our God." Once more branches are cut for those celebrating the feast, the elect hold palms in their hands. It is also probable that the theme of white robes is derived from the feast of the seventh month,[17] although there is no explicit reference to this in the inspired books.

The feast of Tents, as we have seen, was not completely abolished. It was a celebration for the moment when the seed had come to the end of its slow development and the harvest was assured. The author of the Apocalypse took care to relate this eschatological feast to the paschal mystery: in the blood of the lamb the elect washed and whitened their robes! Only regular celebration of Easter will make it possible for us one day to celebrate once more the feast of abundance and life, in which we can recognize the "shepherd who leads us to the waters of life"—this is another basic theme of the feast of the seventh month that appears in the Apocalypse.

17 Cf. Riesenfeld, *op. cit.*

There are other allusions.[18] We have cited only the most significant text, the one that best shows that an important feast is missing from our liturgical calendar and that we cannot celebrate this feast of the final enthronement of the eternal King until, holding palms in our hands, perfectly cleansed by the redemptive blood of the paschal lamb, we are able to celebrate it in all its fullness.

I. CONCLUSION

On the level of cosmic religion, the harvest feast consists essentially of man's appeal to a pre-temporal archetype who, he believes, controls and regulates time. To explain and direct the time-event of the harvest, to be in harmony with it, to understand it and grasp its basic rhythm, lest it escape in some incomprehensible crisis, man discovers behind it its archetype, its controlling "myth." He transcends the cycle of nature in order to reach its origins; this explains his account of first creation with its repetitive cycles, sacred marriages of gods, explanations of lots, etc. But on this level the feast does not make man absolute master of the harvest event: unknown and unsuspected laws disturbed the regular order and the sequence and absolute transparence of the archetype through such events as drought or rain, fruit blight or enemy invasion. Man also attempted to dominate these imponderables. He used magic as his instrument to control what is gratuitous and the result of chance; he sprinkled water as a

[18] For the feast of Tents in apocalyptic symbolism, see Comblin, "La liturgie de la nouvelle Jérusalem," *Eph. Lov.* 1953, pp. 27-40.

prelude to the flow of abundant rain, he drew lots, etc. But it is a fundamental limitation of cosmic religion that it cannot go very far in this direction and must acknowledge the absence of any relation between man and the gratuitous, between the creature and the unforeseeable. The feast of Harvests has not yet attained all the dimensions of the true feast.

When we reach the level of true religion, there is a great change. We find that the Jews, unlike the devotees of cosmic religions, were accustomed to acknowledge the gratuitous and the unforeseeable. Their God comes when He pleases and intervenes through such unusual events as miracles, through such unforeseeable events as revelation, through such gratuitous events as mercy. The archetype par excellence of these gratuitous events is the sojourn in the desert and the economy that this sojourn unfolds. Forever after, whether the harvest be good or bad, it will always be an "event" that the Hebrew people will be able to grasp, with which they can find themselves in perfect harmony, because they know the archetype: the time of testing in the desert and the gratuity of God's election. Whether the harvest be good or bad, the Hebrew knows that forever after it will be an event that will make it possible for him to re-read the events of the desert: when it is good, it will be for him a new manifestation of the "wonders" of the exodus and of the fertility that he once found in the desert; when it is bad, he will look on it as a testing and trial of his fidelity.

We make a mistake if, in the Jewish re-reading that can see the desert tents in the harvest huts and the legendary water rock in the fertilizing libations, we find nothing more than an exercise in subtle symbolism. Behind these interpretations, which we may condemn for their lack of good taste, is the beginning of a spirit of faith that invests the harvest event with new meaning and which suggests moral and spiritual attitudes in keeping with this re-reading.

It must be admitted that in the feast of Tents, the Jewish people did not carry very far the new religious attitudes it inspired in order to assure a new relation between man and the event. Other feasts will carry spiritualization further. But Christ will give a re-reading in which new spiritual elements will appear.

Having taken part in the feast of Tents, as He did on several occasions, He discovered in it a new harmony that He was the first to experience: not only of His being with the rhythm of natural creation, not only the relation of His life with the life of the people in the desert, but something deeper still, the relation of the attitude of His soul with the feast.

Christ, in fact, found Himself in absolute agreement with His Father through His submission and His fidelity, but especially as Creator of everything connected with the celebration of the feast. It is in this sense that He is the rock of living water, that He is the enthroned King, that He is the tree yielding miraculous fruit, that He is the scapegoat. On this level the event becomes a person whose awareness of all this creates and establishes the object of the feast.

On this level of spiritualization, Christ alone is able to celebrate the feast perfectly because He alone is able to say that He creates and establishes the object of the feast. But the time will come when we will share the privilege possessed by the children of God who can themselves create these relations and are so much in control of the events in their sphere of freedom that they can meet Christ on this level. Then the feast of Tents will once more be celebrated. This feast will be eternal. It will constitute the celestial liturgy in which our knowledge will embrace all our acts and our freedom, yet it will not cease to be perfectly gratuitous. Our feast will then consist in our perfect accord with the totally gratuitous event of God's love and the love of all men and we will share in the creation of this event and in the understanding of its establishment.

Chapter Five

the Feast of the First Sheaf or the Feast of the Pasch

A. PRELIMINARIES

So far we have not yet encountered a single Jewish feast that has found a place in the Christian calendar. The feast of the first sheaf, the old feast of spring, is the first feast of the pagan cosmic religions which after a long and gradual process of spiritualization became the Christian feast par excellence, externally a continuation of the ancient man-made feasts but totally renewed in meaning and depth.

Let us briefly recall the human origins of this feast. It was composed of two essential elements, the rite of unleavened bread and the rite of the protecting blood of the lamb.

Even today the rite of the lamb is classic among nomadic tribes. A lamb is immolated, its flesh is not necessarily eaten but its blood is always sprinkled on the tent pegs to ward off evil spirits.[19] As for the azemes rite of the unleavened bread, it seems to have had its origin among agrarian tribes and is an expression of the farmer's anxious care not to mix flour made from new grain and old.[20]

Thus our starting point is a syncretism of the nomadic and agrarian rites that prevailed in the pagan world at the moment when the Hebrew people came into being. The feast was a combination of a spring celebration that for a while seemed to determine the new year, and the ritual of the lamb that protected from evil.

It is understandable that the renewal of spring became concretized in a feast during that season, just as the abundance of the harvest became concretized in a fall festival. If the spring feast never became as important as the fall observance of the Feast of the Tents, it is easy to see why. In the spring hard work in the field limited leisure which was abundantly available after the harvests were gathered.

Our semi-pagans today, who constitute the vast majority of our people, in their own way spontaneously recognize the feast of spring and this is perhaps an uncon-

19 Consult for example Dhorme, *La religion des Hébreux nomades*, p. 208 ff. and Jaussen, *Coutumes des Arabes en pays de Moab*, p. 337 ff.

20 See Cazelles, *Le Code de l'Alliance*, p. 97.

sciously accepted heritage of Christian civilization: they express their sense of renewal, forgetfulness of the old life, flight from the everyday world to "something else" by means of the Easter vacation, Easter outfits, Easter eggs, etc. It is by studying today's springtime pagan rites that we can see how God acted so as to oblige the people to transcend these rites without sacrificing them, and by means of them to celebrate a renewal of spiritual life and the ascent to the new era of the children of God.

If the magic rite of the blood of the protecting lamb has scarcely any equivalents in a world where technology believes it can serve as a substitute for magic in preserving man from the elements, it is still possible to find superstitiously placed horseshoes hanging over a stable door and other totem indications of the confidence of our contemporaries in good-luck symbols. All this is not unrelated to the instinct that once inspired man to sprinkle his tent posts with blood.

It would seem possible to construct a catechesis, using these human realities as a path along which the Christian could be led to the fullness of the paschal mystery. We would see that the essential lines of this catechesis have been provided by God Himself, if we study the stages of His pedagogy in the Bible.

B. COINCIDENCE OF THE TWO RITES

The first question which we would like to examine is the juxtaposition of the agrarian rite of unleavened bread (the azymes) and the nomadic rite of the lamb.[21] Originally the two rites were not related. In fact, each comes from a different world and if the first is connected with the year's unfolding, the second, on the contrary, is connected with uncontrollable events. One places man in harmony with the rhythm of the world and nature; the other places man, as far as this is possible, in harmony with the unexpected—an epidemic, a disaster, etc.

Nevertheless, the oldest texts of the Bible, beginning with Deuteronomy, show these two feasts in a peaceful coexistence. The Passover is observed on the fourteenth Nizan and the feast of Unleavened Bread begins on the next day. Most likely the slow infiltration of Hebrew nomads into the agrarian land of Canaan was largely responsible for this syncretism. But the Bible offers another explanation that we can look at with modern eyes.

When the Israelites were in Egypt, a succession of terrible plagues swept over the land. The announcement of the last one was particularly tragic: the evil spirit (he is called "the destroying angel" in the Bible) is to pass over the people and strike down the first-born. At once the nomadic Jews performed their traditional rite of the strangled lamb and the sprinkling of blood. The Yahwist reports this tradition in his own way, inserting it within a monotheistic pattern of belief and explains that the destroying angel comes according to God's will; he wants

21 We should recall that nomads most probably knew about the azymes since it was the daily bread. This is true today of some Bedouin tribes. Most likely the parallel existence of the nomad and agrarian azymes made possible the fusion of the two feasts.

to make very clear that the Jews, unlike the Egyptians, possessed a rite powerful enough to protect them:

> Moses called all the elders of Israel and said to them, "Go and procure lambs for your families, and slaughter them as Passover victims. Then take a bunch of hyssop, and dipping it in the blood that is in the basin, sprinkle the lintel and the two doorposts with this blood. But none of you shall go outdoors until morning. For the Lord will go by, striking down the Egyptians. Seeing the blood on the lintel and the two doorposts, the Lord will pass over that door and not let the destroyer come into your houses to strike you down. You shall observe this as a perpetual ordinance for yourselves and your descendants (Ex. 12:21-24).

The desire of the editor of this text to purify the traditional rite is plainly evident, but traces of the old ideas of "magic" can be discerned in the prescription not "to go outdoors until morning." The preservative power of the blood seems to be the most important aspect of the rite because the editor refers to it in the strange etymology that he proposes for the word "pasch," declaring that it means that the destroying angel "passed beyond" or "passed before."[22]

In this way God enters an ancient magical rite to show His people by its consequences that He will "save" them from the catastrophe that is about to crush the Egyptians.

It happened, as if by accident, that this intervention took place in the spring. The feast of the first sheaf,

[22] For a recent interpretation of this word, see Coroyer, "L'origine égyptienne du mot Pâcques," *Revue Biblique,* 1955, pp. 481-496. This author believes that "pasch" means a "blow" struck by Yahweh against the Egyptians.

which marked the beginning of the period of unleavened bread, was near. The Yahwist editor saw the fortuitous coincidence of the two rites. He shows, in fact, that the Jews left Egypt at the moment when unleavened bread was being made. But he gave a new meaning to this bread, lifting it from the natural to the historical level. He described it as bread that had no time to rise because it was carried away so quickly by people eager to flee the land of their bondage:

> The Egyptians likewise urged the people on, to hasten their departure from the land; they thought that otherwise they would all die. The people, therefore, took their dough before it was leavened, in their kneading bowls wrapped in their cloaks on their shoulders. . . . The Israelites set out from Rameses for Socchoth, about six hundred thousand men on foot, not counting children. A crowd of mixed ancestry also went up with them, besides their livestock, very numerous flocks and herds. Since the dough they had brought out of Egypt was not leavened, they baked it into unleavened loaves. They had been rushed out of Egypt and had no opportunity even to prepare food for the journey (Ex. 12:32-39).

This text is of special interest because it shows once again how the Hebrew liturgy succeeded in assimilating a rite of agrarian origin. It merely stripped the lamb rite of all traces of magic and placed it in a monotheistic context by introducing Yahweh's destroying angel. Then the agrarian rite was spiritualized by the addition of new references. Unleavened bread ceased to be the sign of the natural cycle of the seasons and the renewal of life that this cycle brings. It now signified an historic event: the hasty departure of the Israelites from Egypt. Thus the rite lost an agrarian and acquired a nomadic meaning; it moved from a natural, primitive meaning to an historical one. We have noted this same process in several of the agrarian rites of the Feast of Tents.[23] The desert experience affected all rites and changed their symbolism. Yet this modification did not mean a complete break with the world of man and of nature in which the rite had developed. The Hebrew rite continued to commemorate spring's renewal but gave this renewal a deeper value. Its object was not merely the coming of new life in nature which is repeated year after year but it also became the new life given to a people who had been saved miraculously from a great misfortune and who were carried from slavery to freedom.

C. RITE AND WORD

The first important legislative document dealing with the Feast of the Passover belongs to one of the oldest strata of Jewish legislation: the covenant code. In clear terms it affirms the historic interpretation of the feast:

> You shall keep the feast of Unleavened Bread. As I have commanded you, you must eat unleavened bread for seven days at the prescribed time in the month of Abib, for it was then that you came out of Egypt (Ex. 23:14-16).

Too much importance should not be attached to the absence of any allusion to the lamb rite in this text. It is significant that the name chosen to designate the feast is "the feast of azymes," an agrarian term, while the name

[23] See pp. 63-69.

"Passover" is more frequently connected with the lamb rite. Let us also note the interesting fact that the legislative text supports its prescription with the words: "for it was then that you came out of Egypt." This stipulation is important because it shows us that an explanation becomes necessary as soon as liturgical symbolism ceases to be merely natural. In fact the rite requires no catechesis as long as it contains self-evident natural symbolism. A contemporary observer taking part in a meal of unleavened bread could easily discover its obvious meaning, especially in the context of those days. But to see in unleavened bread a sign of the departure from Egypt, an initiation or catechesis is needed. This explains the origin of the liturgical catechesis which is usually attached to a rite as its symbolism ceases to be plainly obvious. In other words, when a pagan rite is spiritualized and introduced into our liturgy, it requires an explanatory catchesis. Word is added to rite to define the new meaning. The re-reading of a human rite is possible only by means of the word.

As a matter of fact, from the time of the Yahwist and especially during the Deuteronomist reform, this catechesis became in some ways ritualized in the ceremonial of the paschal family meal:

> Only unleavened bread may be eaten during the seven days; no leaven and nothing leavened may be found in all your territory. On this day you shall explain to your son, "This is because of what the Lord did for me when I came out of Egypt" (Ex. 13:7-8).

The same catechesis was proposed for the lamb rite:

> Thus you must also observe this rite when you have entered the land which the Lord will give you as he promised. When your children ask you, "What does this rite of yours mean?" you shall reply, "This is the Passover sacrifice of the Lord, who passed over the houses of the Israelites in Egypt; when he struck down the Egyptians, he spared our houses" (Ex. 12:25-27).

The dialogue introduced between the children of the family and their father in connection with the two paschal rites is the origin of the liturgical catechesis. It is the reference to the event that assures the new authenticity of the rite and it is the word that gives the rite its new meaning. We are at the beginning of an evolution that will continue and will become sacred in a fundamental law of Christian liturgical celebrations: the union of word and rite. It was not until after the Counter-Reformation, when Catholics were deprived of the Bible, that they were also deprived of the biblical catechesis of their rites. As a result, for centuries rites were celebrated without catechesis and were often understood, no longer according to their supernatural signification, but according to their human symbolism.[24]

D. THE RITE AND THE ACTUALIZATION OF THE EVENT

Shortly after Solomon's reign there was a marked relaxation in the customs and religion of the Chosen People.

24 For example, the sacrament of Confirmation is explained in terms of the oil needed to run an engine, rather than the oil used to anoint David or Christ, etc.

Past events were forgotten and rites were reduced to a natural, even a pagan meaning. Men referred to the cult of the golden calf, the Baals, the gods of the elements. It will be recalled that the efforts of the prophets from Elias to Isaias to purify the cult from all pagan symbolism proved vain. Not until King Josiah and the Deuteronomist reform were the first steps taken towards spiritualization. In a somewhat draconian and not too successful manner, Josiah insisted that all come to Jerusalem to celebrate the Passover. He thus prevented the perpetuation of pagan customs which might have developed into local celebrations, and by unifying the cult he purified it. But it was above all the actualization of the event commemorated by the rite which was stressed by the Deuteronomist reform. It is easy to see why this was necessary. The Hebrews had gradually lost sight of what had happened in the desert and a comfortable life in a fertile land led them away from desert spirituality. Everything connected with that phase of their past seemed remote and they preferred to accept a natural religion that guaranteed a fruitful soil and regular harvests. To correct these deviations and to revive interest in ancient events, the Deuteronomist declared that the rite not only recalled past events but situated the faithful here and now in the event. The rite did not commemorate an experience which decreased in interest as it receded in time but placed the individual of today in contact with the event.

We have already seen catechetical texts that illustrate this point of view: "it is because of what Yahweh did for *me,"* or "it was during this month that *you* came out of Egypt." But the Deuteronomist gave final consecration to this catechetical form which connects rite and event, and which involves one in that past event:

> Observe the month of Abib by keeping the Passover of the Lord, your God, since it was in the month of Abib that he brought you by night out of Egypt. You shall offer the Passover sacrifice from your flock or your herd to the Lord, your God, in the place which he chooses as the dwelling place of his name. You shall not eat leavened bread with it. For seven days you shall eat with it only unleavened bread, the bread of affliction, that you may remember as long as you live the day of your departure from the land of Egypt; for in frightened haste you left the land of Egypt. Nothing leavened may be found in all your territory for seven days, and none of the meat which you sacrificed on the evening of the first day shall be kept overnight for the next day. You may not sacrifice the Passover in any of the communities which the Lord, your God, gives you; only at the place which he chooses as the dwelling place of his name, and in the evening at sunset, on the anniversary of your departure from Egypt . . . (Deut. 16:1-7).

Many of these passages are simply extracted from early legislative codes, but the creative insight of the Deuteronomist is clearly evident in the care with which the encounter is established for the believer: It is *you* who came out of Egypt.

This information discloses something important about Jewish calendars: the feast places the individual in contact with the event not so much through its symbolism, but rather by recreating in the believer the same attitude as that of his ancestors when they were experiencing this event. In other words, the common denominator between the event and the feast is assured not primarily by the ritual symbolism that recalls this or that event, but by a similar attitude of soul between the ancestor and the believer who relives the historical event.

In today's *Haggadah* of the feast of the Passover, the ritual makes this very clear:

> It was not only our ancestors whom he delivered, but when he delivered them he delivered us with them, because it was not one enemy alone who rose up against us to crush us. The Holy One—blessed be he—rescues us from their hand.

The feast, on this purified level, seeks to create, through the commemoration of the event and the symbolism of the rite, an attitude of soul and a position of faith. In the last analysis it is this that characterizes the essential object of the feast.

The "personalization" of the feast was not, however, achieved at the cost of the symbolism of the rite: on the contrary, continuity with preceding stages was well assured and the symbolism contributed to a further spiritualization. In fact, if the biblical text is taken as a guide it would seem that at this time a new rite was introduced into the feast of the Passover: namely, the eating of the paschal lamb. Possibly the people had begun this custom long before the reform of Josiah, perhaps it was adopted because of local conditions, but the first legal text to make the paschal lamb meal official is found in Deuteronomy:

> Only at the place which he chooses as the dwelling place of his name, and in the evening at sunset, on the anniversary

> of your departure from Egypt, shall you sacrifice the Passover. You shall cook and eat it at the place the Lord, your God, chooses; then in the morning you may return to your tents (Deut. 16:6-7).

Before this time the rite consisted merely in the immolation of the lamb and the sprinkling of its blood on the lintels of the door. If, on certain occasions, the lamb was eaten, the meal formed no part of the paschal rite which was simply a meal of unleavened bread. But after the days of the Deuteronomist, as we see in the sacerdotal code, the paschal lamb meal became more important. This evolution reveals the importance of the personal element. No longer does the symbolism of the rite matter most (that is, the repetition of what was done in time long past) but rather the attitude of soul that the memory of the event recalls. In this light, the eating of the lamb better expresses the personal participation of the faithful in the feast than did the immolation of the lamb. It should also be observed that the Deuteronomist legislation no longer requires that the blood be sprinkled on tent pegs or door lintels: to eat a lamb—and in this way to eat the lamb of the original event—supposes and signifies a far deeper, personal involvement.

When the sacerdotal legislation was in full force, it seemed very much like a compilation of many different elements: lamb and unleavened bread, the rite of the sprinkling of blood and the eating, etc. But there is nothing new in all this legislation, apart from the detailed ceremonial of the meal:

> . . . On the tenth of this month every one of your families must procure for itself a lamb, one apiece for each household. If a family is too small for a whole lamb, it shall join the nearest household in procuring one and shall share in the lamb in proportion to the number of persons who partake of it. The lamb must be a year-old male and without blemish. You may take it from either the sheep or the goats. You shall keep it until the fourteenth day of this month, and then, with the whole assembly of Israel present, it shall be slaughtered during the evening twilight. They shall take some of its blood and apply it to the two doorposts and the lintel of every house in which they partake of the lamb. That same night they shall eat its roasted flesh with unleavened bread and bitter herbs. It shall not be eaten raw or boiled, but roasted whole, with its head and shanks and inner organs. None of it must be kept beyond the next morning; whatever is left over in the morning shall be burned up. This is how you are to eat it: with your loins girt, sandals on your feet and your staff in hand, you shall eat like those who are in flight. It is the Passover of the Lord (Ex. 12:3-12).

For the moment let us ignore the minor details of the ritual so that we may concentrate only on the essential. When the faithful Jew stood like a nomad and ate the paschal lamb, he meant to do much more than to recall the past event which the rite symbolized. He wished to make his own the attitude of his ancestors, to enter into their act of liberation, to share in their interior life. This is why the meal marks an advance over the ancient rite of immolation and the sprinkling of blood.

So we see the rich evolution of the Passover feast down to our day. First, a catechesis had to be introduced, then the paschal meal required an informed, personal awareness. This meant it became a means of reliving the salvific event in the measure in which the believer drew near in faith. The rite recalled the salvific event, making it present and, as it were, enabled the participant to adhere and consent to all that it meant. Here we have the beginning and the meaning of the *Hodie* of our Christian liturgy.

E. THE FEAST OF THE RESTORATION OF THE PEOPLE

Our investigations of the feast of Tents and of the feasts of the astronomical order did not reveal as much personification as we find in the Passover feast. It was probably the presence of this dynamic principle that assured the survival of this feast and enabled it, unlike so many other Jewish feasts, to meet the exacting demands of Christianity.

The pre-eminence of the Passover can be discerned even in the Old Testament, at a time when the feast of Tents was still "the feast" par excellence. Thus, at various moments in the history of the Chosen People when a restoration was to reaffirm or seal once again the Covenant which they had so often endangered by their infidelities, the reformers naturally thought of the Passover and not of the feast of Tents as the occasion for covenant renewal and restoration. Josiah first solemnly proclaimed the renewal of the Covenant, then sealed this act with the celebration of the paschal feast:

> And he commanded all the people, saying: "Keep the phase to the Lord your God, according as it is written in the book

> of this covenant." Now there was no such a phase kept from the days of the judges, who judged Israel, nor in all the days of the kings of Israel, and of the kings of Juda, as was this phase that was kept to the Lord in Jerusalem, in the eighteenth year of King Josias (4 Kings 23:21-23).

In this way the moral aspect became central, in order to assure the value of the covenant renewal which Josiah had sealed, and at the same time the feast of the Passover was restored. At a later date, Esdras celebrated the Passover to mark the completion of the post-exilic restoration.

> And the children of Israel of the captivity kept the phase, on the fourteenth day of the first month. For all the priests and the Levites were purified as one man: all were clean to kill the phase for all the children of the captivity, and for their brethren the priests, and themselves. And the children of Israel that were returned from captivity, and all that had separated themselves from the filthiness of the nations of the earth to them, to seek the Lord the God of Israel, did eat. And they kept the feast of unleavened bread seven days with joy; . . . (Es. 6:19-22).

The personal attitude, which is here an attitude of conversion, is now the most important element of the feast.

Shortly after the exile, the priestly documents record still another important Passover, the one that King Ezechiah celebrated when the Covenant was renewed. The books of Kings showed no interest in this feast, for which the people had probably not been prepared. On the contrary, the books of Chronicles, due to the deuteronomical and especially to the priestly influence, attached great importance to its restoration. They describe in great detail how this feast was celebrated in the second month instead of the first to assure the perfect purification of the people (2 Chr. 30).[25]

It is also possible that the chroniclers projected back to the days of Ezechiel a fact that must have originated during Josiah's reform. The same spirit of anticipation is found in the description of the first Passover celebration by the people when they reached Galgal (Jos. 5:10-12). This account is undoubtedly an ancient one but it was reread in the light of sacerdotal preoccupations.

So we see that the attitude of soul on the individual plane and the restoration and renewal of the covenant on the collective plane, made the Passover more and more into a personal feast whose essential purpose was an attitude of soul, conversion, moral fidelity. To this the rite made an important contribution. It included many references to the past: the loaves of unleavened bread were still used and recalled the springtime renewal that was now transcended by the moral renewal. The blood of the lamb recalled the liberation from Egypt and this commemoration was still the true purpose of the feast, but a purpose subject to repeated rereadings by men called to conversion and to an ever deeper interior renewal.

Ezechiel's *Torah* reports a final modification of the Passover ritual. An expiation ceremony was now ob-

[25] At the same time it justified the creation of a minor Passover celebration in the second month for those who did not have an opportunity to take part in the first celebration.

served before the feast. This duplicated the old expiation feast connected with the feast of Tents and is indicative of the decline of this feast and the relative increase in importance of the Passover, especially the enhancement of its personal and moral values. If our ancestors moved from Egypt into the Promised Land, we should now celebrate this feast by moving from impurity to purity:

> Thus saith the Lord God: "In the first month, the first of the month, thou shalt take a calf of the herd without blemish, and thou shalt expiate the sanctuary. And the priest shall take of the blood of the sin offering: and he shall put it on the posts of the house and on the four corners of the brim of the altar and on the posts of the gate of the inner court. And so shalt thou do in the seventh day of the month, for everyone that hath been ignorant and hath been deceived by error . . ." (Ez. 45:18-20).

In this passage we see that a new theme has been introduced: the expiatory victim duplicates the liberating paschal lamb. Soon a single person will assume both roles in His unique sacrifice. He will be both the scapegoat and the paschal lamb.

F. PASSOVER AND THE PERPETUAL CALENDAR

Not until the priestly documents were composed was the Passover assigned a definite date. The earlier texts we have cited merely refer to "the time fixed in the month of Abib" (Ex. 23:15). Even the Deuteronomist fails to be specific:

> Observe the month of Abib by keeping the Passover of the Lord, your God, since it was in the month of Abib that he brought you by night out of Egypt. You shall offer the Passover sacrifice from your flock or your herd to the Lord, your God, in the place which he chooses as the dwelling place of his name (Deut. 16:1-2).

This vagueness is understandable because the date of the feast was determined by the beginning of the barley harvest and the offering of the first sheaf. The word "Abib" itself means "ear." But as the rite of the lamb gradually became more important than the rite of the barley ear and the unleavened bread, the feast was freed from too servile a dependence on agrarian cycles and acquired its own personality. Moreover, as long as the calendar was based on the phases of the moon, the feast might fall on any day of the week. After the Exile, in some priestly circles, a new way of computing time was devised, partly lunar, partly solar. Reactions were lively but it was now possible to determine definite dates and hereafter all biblical time references are stated with precision, even to the month and the day.

The new type of calendar was a perpetual solar calendar with some concession to lunar cycles. Thus it was agreed that the fourteenth Nizan (the new date for Easter) would never fall before the full moon of that month. Here is Mlle. Jaubert's reconstruction of this calendar.[26] With it we can follow later developments in the Jewish liturgy.

[26] Jaubert, *La date de la Cène,* Gabalda, 1957.

MONTHS	I, IV, VII, X		II, V, VIII, XI		III, VI, IX, XII	
DAYS	1 W	16 Th	1 F	16 S	1 S	16 M
	2 Th	17 Fr	2 S	17 S	2 M	17 T
	3 Fr	18 S	3 S	18 M	3 T	18 W
	4 S	19 S	4 M	19 T	4 W	19 Th
	5 S	20 M	5 T	20 W	5 Th	20 F
	6 M	21 T	6 W	21 Th	6 F	21 S
	7 T	22 W	7 Th	22 F	7 S	22 S
	8 W	23 Th	8 F	23 S	8 S	23 M
	9 Th	24 F	9 S	24 S	9 M	24 T
	10 F	25 S	10 S	25 M	10 T	25 W
	11 S	26 S	11 M	26 T	11 W	26 Th
	12 S	27 M	12 T	27 W	12 Th	27 F
	13 M	28 T	13 W	28 Th	13 F	28 S
	14 T	29 W	14 Th	29 F	14 S	29 S
	15 W	30 Th	15 F	30 S	15 S	30 M
						31 T

All post-exilic dates in biblical documents are calculated according to this calendar. Therefore, the Passover always falls on the evening of the fourteenth Nizan (i.e., first month). This is always a Tuesday, and the feast continues the next day which is always Wednesday, the fifteenth Nizan. But it need not be supposed that this calendar won universal support. The temple priests clung to or returned to the old calendar, in which the Passover fell in different years on different days of the week, according to the phases of the moon.

In fact it seems that the perpetual calendar was accepted only in certain Jewish communities in Palestine,

Babylon and Elephantine.[27] Eventually only those who belonged to special sects, such as the Qumran community, followed this calendar which was opposed in many ways to the one used in the temple of Jerusalem, at least at the time of Christ. In every religion, calendars have been the object of bitter quarrels so it is not too surprising that this is also true of the Chosen People. One of the arguments in support of the perpetual calendar deserves our attention. Its partisans claimed that those who followed a lunar calendar were observing one that was pagan in origin and was largely responsible for the syncretism of Jewish and pagan customs. Such an argument has some foundation and it is possible that a special calendar was constructed for the express purpose of stressing the originality of Jewish feasts and liturgy.

The calendar question was further complicated by the insertion of the Passover. Two of these repercussions contributed to the spiritualization of the feast as we shall now see.

First, let us note that as a result of the change, the Passover was to be celebrated hereafter in "the first month of the year."[28] So it was this feast, and not the feast of Tents, that was privileged to inaugurate the new year.

27 Cf. Grelot, "Etudes sur le Papyrus pascal d'Eléphantine," *V.T.*, 1954, 349-384; "Le papyrus pascal et le problème du Pentateuque," *ibid.*, 1955, p. 250 ff.

28 It was probably due to Babylonian influence that the Jews decided to change their calendar some time around the year 600. Probably it was then that they changed certain dates and calculations.

> This month shall stand at the head of your calendar; you shall reckon it the first month of the year (Ex. 12:2).
> The Passover of the Lord falls on the fourteenth day of the first month, at the evening twilight. The fifteenth day of this month is the Lord's feast of Unleavened Bread (Lev. 23:5-6).

In these prescriptions we should see an important consecration of the evolution that had made the Passover the most spiritual of all the feasts of the Jewish cycle. Certain prerogatives of the feast of Tents had been or were at this time transferred to the feast of the Passover. The opening of the new year was not changed just as the feast of expiation had been. In this perspective, it is easy to understand why early Christian tradition continued in this same spirit and moved the ceremony of the enthronement of the messiah from the feast of Tents to the feast of the Passover, in connection with Christ's entry into Jerusalem.[29]

The second change, even though it be a hypothetical one, deserves our closest attention. Since there were two different ways of calculating the date of the Passover—that proposed in the official temple calendar based on the moon and the sectarian one based on the perpetual calendar—does it not follow that these were two ways of celebrating the paschal meal? It is hard to believe that those who followed the perpetual calendar, in which the Passover fell on Tuesday evening, would eat the paschal lamb according to the old rubrics which required that the lamb

[29] Cf. *Supra*, pp. 89-92.

be immolated in the temple by priests who were following another calendar which placed the immolation of the lamb a few days later. It is possible that they celebrated the feast without any paschal lamb and this would not be too surprising.[30] Possibly the Qumran monks immolated a paschal lamb, but instead of going to the temple they may have decided that their own community, because of its charity and mutual service, was a true temple (a fundamental Qumran doctrine) and gave them the right to immolate a lamb there.

This is an attractive hypothesis. It could well constitute a new stage in the spiritualization of the Passover and be a direct preparation for Christ's action at His own paschal meal. The lamb has become no more than a symbol of an attitude of soul. As soon as this attitude exists—and it does exist where there is a spirit of mutual service (especially if the lamb is seen as the symbol of "the Servant")—certain ritual precepts connected with the immolation of the lamb can give way to the essential meaning of the rite and disappear. We shall return later to the importance of this spiritualization.

A similar problem is connected with the azymes. If there were two concurrent calendars, it is likely that there was confusion about the Passover ritual. Those who followed the perpetual calendar sometimes ate the paschal meal even though the feast of the azymes had not preceded it, unless some special provision was made for this

30 After the destruction of the temple, the custom had spread of not eating the paschal lamb until the temple was rebuilt.

in the official temple calendar. So it may be that Christ celebrated the Last Supper during the evening of Tuesday, the fourteenth Nizan, without any lamb (which would not be immolated in the temple until the following Friday) and even without unleavened bread. It is precisely this point that we shall try to understand in the following section.

G. CHRIST IN THE PASCHAL CELEBRATION

This digression about the calendar quarrel has not been futile. It enables us, in the light of Mlle. Jaubert's work,[31] to understand more clearly Christ's action at the Passover and to see to what an extraordinary degree He made that feast His own.

The best explanation that can be given of the apparent contradictions between the synoptics and John in regard to the chronology of Holy Week is to be found in the conflict of two different calendars. This disagreement continued in the early Christian church and was in part responsible for the grave paschal quarrels that divided Christendom until the third century.

In the year of the Last Supper, the Passover of the fourteenth Nizan fell, according to the perpetual calendar, on Tuesday, but the Passover according to the lunar

31 See for favorable reactions: Delorme, "La Cène et Pâques," *Lumière et Vie,* 31, pp. 9-48; "Jésus a-t-il pris la Cène le mardi soir?" *Ami du Clergé,* 1957, p. 218. Some exegetes, however, reject Mlle. Jaubert's reasoning (Jérémias, Benôit). Yet almost all agree with Mlle. Jaubert that the Last Supper was an ordinary meal to which Christ gave a paschal meaning. This would seem to us to justify our position.

calendar, as observed in the temple, fell on the following Friday. Christ celebrated the paschal meal with His Apostles on Tuesday evening, therefore without a lamb and probably without unleavened bread. He died on Friday, at the exact hour when the paschal lamb was being immolated in the temple, as John discreetly notes. At the present time, many Holy Week excerpts accept these facts.

But what is the value for our purpose of a paschal meal without a lamb or unleavened bread? Does this not negate the evolution of this feast? Or, on the contrary, does this omission mark its culmination?

One point must be stressed: After the Exile, the Passover became the feast of the renewal of an attitude of soul, the feast of the "restoration." Each one renews his love and fidelity, and this renewal is made explicit in the eating of the paschal meal. The important coordinates of the feast are not those that relate the rite and its symbolism to the past event that is being commemorated, but on the contrary, those that relate the rite to the present attitude of the believing soul.

Now it came to pass that one of the faithful, Christ, the faithful one par excellence, celebrated the Passover with a very definite attitude of soul: so definite that it became *the* event of the whole history of salvation: an attitude of submission to His Father, a desire to "serve" His brothers by His expiatory death. So essential is this event that all other rites disappear, become unnecessary, cease to be. No need to immolate a lamb because the

Lamb of God is there in Person, like the Servant of God (cf. Is. 53:7), offering Himself for the sins of the world, giving Himself as food.

For this reason it is understandable that Christ chose the perpetual calendar rather than the lunar calendar for the Last Supper. In this way He freed Himself more easily from constraining rites and could the better present Himself as both rite and event. The rite had a meaning in the absence of the event that it was meant to recall; it had no meaning in the event itself.

The deepest meaning of Christ's paschal meal is no longer found in its ritual but in the Lord's attitude of soul which He tried to communicate to His Apostles. In this connection it is interesting to compare the different rites of the paschal meal as recorded in the gospels and in the words of Paul. Matthew and Mark go no further than a description of the institution of the new rite in which bread and wine are central. But Luke introduces a curious quarrel between the Apostles which the other synoptics place at another moment in Christ's life:

> Now there arose also a dispute among them, which of them was reputed to be the greatest. But he said to them, "The Kings of the Gentiles lord it over them, and they who exercise authority over them are called Benefactors. But not so with you. On the contrary, let him who is greatest among you become as the youngest, and him who is the chief as the servant. For which is the greater, he who reclines at table, or he who serves? Is it not he who reclines? But I am in your midst as he who serves" (Lk. 22:24-27).

Luke certainly had a reason for introducing or retaining this tradition in his account of the Last Supper.

It enables us to see and properly value this incident: the presence of a humble and suffering "servant" is sufficient in itself to justify the celebration of the Passover because it is its content.

John goes still further when he replaces the whole account of the institution of the washing of the feet, and makes the latter an essential element of the paschal meal:

> And during the supper, the devil having already put it into the heart of Judas Iscariot, the son of Simon, to betray him, Jesus, knowing that the Father had given all things into his hands, and that he had come forth from God and was going to God, rose from the supper and laid aside his garments, and taking a towel girded himself. Then he poured water into the basin and began to wash the feet of the disciples, and to dry them with the towel with which he was girded. . . . Now after he had washed their feet and put on his garments, when he had reclined again, he said to them, "Do you know what I have done to you? You call me Master and Lord, and you say well, for so I am. If, therefore, I the Lord and Master have washed your feet, you also ought to wash the feet of one another. For I have given you an example, that as I have done to you, so you also should do. Amen, amen, I say to you, no servant is greater than his master, nor is one who is sent greater than he who sent him" (Jn. 13:2-16).

Perhaps a significant change was also made in regard to the bread. It is possible that Christ used ordinary instead of unleavened bread to signify His Body. The word "aptos" seems to suggest this, as well as the earlier day of the week chosen for the paschal meal.

It is easy to see to what extent Jesus transformed the rites of the Passover feast. He adopted another calendar. He did not use the two elements that had always been essential to the rite: the lamb and the unleavened bread. In doing this He made it possible for Christian communities to celebrate the Passover every Sunday. At the same time He made very clear the reality that these rites signify. The lamb's expiatory and liberating blood is still there, but under the form of a servant and in the drama of a humbled person. All the newness of the springtime feast is still there, but under the form of the "new" covenant sealed by this blood. Although unleavened bread is no longer used, all that it signified of fresh beginnings and flight from the past remains so essentially part of the new paschal rite that Paul can allude to these things without seeming to be looking backward:

> Purge out the old leaven, that you may be a new dough, as you really are without leaven. For Christ, our passover, has been sacrificed. Therefore, let us keep festival, not with the old leaven, nor with the leaven of malice and wickedness, but with the unleavened bread of sincerity and truth (1 Cor. 5:7-8).

From this text we can see how the Passover should now be celebrated. Christ's attitude of soul enabled Him to personalize the feast within the drama of His own experience. It is also our own attitude of soul during our participation that becomes the content of the feast: the rite of the unleavened bread becomes our renunciation of evil and our new covenant with God, just as the rite of the lamb became Christ Himself.

Nevertheless the right perdures, even in the celebration of the Christian Passover:

> For as often as you shall eat this bread and drink the cup, you proclaim the death of the Lord until he comes. Therefore whoever eats this bread or drinks the cup of the Lord unworthily, will be guilty of the body and blood of the Lord (1 Cor. 11:26-27).

Thus today, although the attitude of the faithful soul united to the attitude of Christ-the-Servant is the essential content of the feast of the Passover, the rite still continues, both as the objective presence of Christ and of His attitude of soul and also as an occasion capable of arousing in us a corresponding attitude of soul. Henceforth, the Passover can be celebrated in a new way in which the rite retains none of the magic meaning of days long ago, nor even its old symbolic value, but has become a sacrament; that is, it contains the act of Christ Himself who is the object of the feast and, at the same time, it includes the act of the believer who renews with Christ the eternal covenant which His act inspires.

H. A CHRISTIAN PASCHAL HOMILY

We have pointed out that liturgical catechesis was introduced to accompany the rite as soon as the spiritualization of the feast advanced beyond its purely natural symbolism. It would seem reasonable to suppose that the liturgical catechesis would be even more important when the rite became part of Christian worship and both expressed and realized the new event of Christ and the corresponding attitude of the believer. In this connection we are particularly fortunate because we possess an apostolic homily in Peter's first letter. It has recently been analyzed and shown to be a composition containing parenetic material including a catechetical booklet for the paschal-night celebration.[32] An examination of the most characteristic notes of this study will suffice to show the degree to which the feast of the Passover was purified and what concrete demands it made in the lives of those who celebrated it.

If we disregard the letter's heading, which was added later so that the homily might be included among the epistles of the New Testament, we read first of all an introductory hymn to the paschal-night liturgy which Father Boismard, using parallel texts such as Titus 3:5-7, has restored as follows:

> Blessed be the God and Father of our Lord Jesus Christ, who according to his great mercy has begotten us again, through the resurrection of Jesus Christ, from the dead, into a living hope, unto an incorruptible inheritance—undefiled and unfading, reserved for you in heaven (1 Pet. 1:3-5).

After this entrance blessing, we may suppose that it was customary to read Exodus 12, a practice which is certainly a heritage from Judaism and is found in all paschal liturgies. The story of the Jewish event and the description of the paschal meal enabled the Jews to unite themselves to this event and make it their own.

Then 1 Peter furnishes us with the points of a Christian homily on this Jewish reading (1 Pet. 1:13-21). This homily-plan is particularly interesting because it shows us how the ceremony leads to an attitude of soul.

32 Boismard, *Revue Biblique,* 1956, pp. 183-190. These opinions we have adopted with slight modifications.

First of all, this is what becomes of the rite of girt loins prescribed in the meal ceremonial:

> Therefore, having girded up the loins of your understanding, be sober and set your hope completely upon that grace which is brought to you in the revelation of Jesus Christ (1 Pet. 1:13).

The rite of the lamb is in its turn spiritualized (Ex. 12:5):

> You know that you were redeemed from the vain manner of life handed down from your fathers, not with perishable things, with silver or gold, but with the precious blood of Christ, as of a lamb without blemish and without spot (1 Pet. 1:18-19).

Both the departure from Egypt and the worship to be paid to Yahweh in the desert (Ex. 12:31), are also to be handled in a spiritual way: Idols are to be abandoned and worship is to be made in spirit and in truth.

> As obedient children, do not conform to the lusts of former days when you were ignorant; but as the One who called you is holy, be you also holy in all your behavior; for it is written, "You shall be holy, because I am holy" (1 Pet. 1:14-15).

The attitude of the Christian soul is the fulfillment of the rite. But this attitude of soul is inspired and fostered by the sacramental rite. According to Father Boismard, the homily is followed by the baptism of the new Christians. After this ceremony, another homily (an outline is provided in 1 Peter) explains the mystery of the sacrament.

This homily is in the form of a diptych: a short mystagogical catechesis and a moral exhortation. First, let us examine the catechesis:

> Now that your obedience to charity has purified your souls for a brotherly love that is sincere, love one another heartily and intensely. For you have been reborn, not from corruptible seed but from incorruptible, through the word of God who lives and abides forever. . . . Crave as newborn babes, pure spiritual milk, that by it you may grow to salvation; if, indeed, you have tasted that the Lord is sweet (1 Pet. 1:22-2:3).

The emphasis here is on the idea of the new birth and the passage from the corruptible to the incorruptible. In this new birth must be noted the importance of the "word" which is at the same time the Person of Christ and the Person of the Spirit, in the teaching of the Church: Baptism is "a bath of water accompanied by a word" as Paul says (Eph. 5:26) as if to make clear where the originality of the Christian rite is to be found. There is certainly a rite but it is accompanied by a word of God and by obedience to this word.

Catechesis continues in a more ecclesial vein. Central in the life of a new people must be sacrifice and the spiritual priesthood:

> Draw near to him, a living stone, rejected indeed by men but chosen and honored by God. Be you yourselves as living stones, built thereon into a spiritual house, a holy priesthood, to offer spiritual sacrifices acceptable to God through Jesus Christ. . . . You, however, are a chosen race, a royal priesthood, a holy nation, a purchased people; that you may proclaim the perfections of him who has called you out of darkness into his marvellous light. You who in times past

were not a people, but are now the people of God; who had not obtained mercy, but now have obtained mercy (1 Pet. 2:4-10).

The purpose of this text is to show that the Church inherits the privileges of the Jewish people. To the paschal event that established their privileges, now corresponds the Person and the mystery of Christ who makes into a people those who are grafted into His life and are joined to Him, the foundation stone, in the new building.

The importance of the theme of the Spirit must also be observed. All is "spiritual" here. The feast of the Passover introduces us into the eschatological reality marked precisely by the gift of the Spirit. This is directly connected with baptism "according to the Spirit," which has just been celebrated.

As soon as this catechesis is over, there is a moral exhortation that seems to apply the themes of new birth and spiritual life to daily life. All the social categories of the newly baptized are reviewed so as to show how Christians should behave (1 Pet. 2.11-3:12).

The celebration concludes with a new hymn that has been reconstructed along these lines and seems to have been inspired by the Jewish theme of the two ways:

God resists the proud,
but gives grace to the humble.
Humble yourselves, therefore, under the mighty hand of God,
that he may exalt you
in the time of visitation,

cast all your anxiety upon him,
because he cares for you (1 Pet. 5:6-7).

Father Boismard and those exegetes who claim that Peter's letter is a paschal homily may prove to have applied their thesis too rigorously. Yet it must be admitted that this Epistle contains a particularly impressive set of hymns and parenetic documents that are strikingly unified around the paschal feast. But what is even more significant is the profound modification achieved within the primitive Christian milieu on certain ancient elements of the Passover feast. The Person of the Lord Himself is central in the celebration. He is the Word that accompanies the rite, the Word that is the "revelation" of God's plan in the rite and that attracts the believer's "obedience."

I. CONCLUSION

We might examine our way of celebrating the Passover today in the light of all that God has done to realize His ideal Passover. Do we really situate ourselves at the sacramental level where, in the rite, our faith meets Christ's attitude or are we satisfied with the emotion generated by the paschal symbolism? Are we still on the level of the simple historical commemoration or do we merely observe a rite having a certain "magical" content?

These questions deserve to be asked. If a serious examination of conscience shows that the liturgical reforms decreed by the Church recently do not bear fruit or are marked by a certain lassitude, may it not be because pastors and faithful do not understand them?

In this connection it is striking to follow the decline of Easter in the history of the Church and to discover the various reasons for this. During the early centuries, most of Easter night was spent in baptisms and the Eucharist. This was fully within the sacramental realm. The paschal rite, be it baptismal or eucharistic, mobilized the whole community (not only the neophytes) in an attitude of conversion, in a communal and deliberate profession of faith which affirmed one's desire to join Christ in His new, risen life. Previously, the community fasted, the better to be united to His acceptance of death. At that time there were no special ceremonies apart from the rites connected with the administration of the sacraments. Everything was to be found in the interior renewal produced by those sacraments in connection with Christ's paschal event.

The disappearance of Baptisms from the paschal vigil marked the inauguration of the second period. Two rites were then introduced whose meaning was symbolic rather than directly sacramental. The blessing of water was expanded out of all proportion and was substituted for Baptisms that were no longer celebrated; water, as something symbolic, replaced the sacrament and the living act of conversion. In the same way the blessing of light (the paschal candle) was expanded, precisely at the moment when the vigil was anticipated earlier and earlier so that light was less and less needed. Of course, there was plenty of opportunity to proclaim the paschal mystery in connection with the symbols of water and light and to arouse the indispensable attitude of soul. But was this always done?

During a third period, which paralleled the second, the rites were given an historical content. Men lost sight of the fact that the rite actualized the past and made it instead a memorial of the past, just as the first Jews celebrated the Passover in memory of the liberation from Egypt. Thus they "mimed" the Resurrection with the paschal candle's abrupt apparition in the dark church, and they did the same for Christ's entrance into Jerusalem with the procession of palms and the washing of the feet. Here again, catechesis, which can make a fine fire with almost any kind of wood, could have made good use of these historical rites to rediscover the essential. Instead an effort was made to arouse emotional rather than truly Christian reactions, as for example, in the "mime" which we call the stations of the cross and in the adoration of the cross.

During the fourth and last period, the ritual content of Easter sank to a still lower level. Here we must refer to the theme of fire which leaps from the rock that is Christ (a way of counteracting similar magical rites in the German world), bits of the paschal candle which were carried home in the form of sacramentals and which in time became our present day *Agnus Dei,* a big supply of blessed water, on Holy Saturday the endless blessing of branches, etc.

As we make this rapid survey of the history of the decline of the feast, does there not seem to be some kind of a movement in reverse of God's successive Old Testament purifications of the Jewish feast of the Passover? And even though there has occurred a happy reform of the paschal vigil, does it not ultimately depend on the way priests catechize the faithful, if this reform is to succeed in reestablishing a real paschal feast in which the renewal of Christ is made present in the midst of a community of believers who are fully aware of what is taking place and who, through the sacraments, renew both their faith and their conversion so that all may become more truly children of God?

Chapter Six

the Feast of the Sheaf of Wheat or the Feast of Pentecost

The feast of Pentecost, it would seem, was celebrated from the earliest days of the Jewish people but it remained for many years in the background. Increasing attention paid to the feast of the Passover made it more important, thanks, in part, to a matter of mathematics. In spite of all this, the feast of Pentecost acquired its own characteristics and was worthy of becoming part of the Christian liturgy.

The study of the evolution of the feast of Pentecost in the Jewish world is particularly difficult, precisely because the feast was never as important as the feast of the Passover or of Tents. Biblical references to the feast are scanty, and it is only later Jewish history that gives interesting evidence for it—and even this material should be used with caution.

A. THE AGRARIAN FEAST

The oldest biblical texts retain the old name: the feast of Harvests:

> You shall also keep the feast of the grain harvest with the first of the crop that you have sown in the field . . . (Ex. 23:16).
> You shall keep the feast of Weeks with the first of the wheat harvest; likewise the feast at the fruit harvest . . . (Ex. 34:22).

The first text that we have just cited is part of the old covenant code that may go back to Moses. The second is more recent because it is in a Yahwist section. It seems to have been retouched and corrected by a later hand because the feast is given two names: the feast of Weeks and the feast of Harvests. Let us leave aside for a moment the first title and concentrate on the agrarian aspect which we know well. In the month of May, the "third month" of the year, according to recent Jewish calculations, the harvests were ready to be gathered in Palestine.[33] This feast was meant to complete and bless them just as the feast of Tents blessed the harvests in the month of September.

33 Cf. Gen. 30:14; Judg. 15:1; 1 Kgs. 6:13; 12:17, where we see the importance of harvests in Israel.

It is difficult for us to place a proper value on this feast. At least we can say that the legislative texts that we have just quoted include it among the three great feasts of the year which the Deuteronomist reform made the axis of the whole liturgical year. Since these feasts involved a pilgrimage to Jerusalem, agreement had to be reached as to the dates of their celebration. Therefore, Deuteronomy provided data that made it possible to calculate the date of the Passover and the harvest feasts:

> You shall count off seven weeks, computing them from the day when the sickle is first put to the standing grain. You shall then keep the feast of Weeks in honor of the Lord, your God, and the measure of your own free will offering shall be in proportion to the blessing the Lord, your God, has bestowed on you. In the place which the Lord, your God, chooses as the dwelling place of his name, you shall make merry in his presence together with your son and daughter, your male and female slave, and the Levite who belongs to your community, as well as the alien, the orphan and widow among you. Remember that you too were once slaves in Egypt, and carry out these statutes carefully (Deut. 16:9-12).

This is still an essentially agrarian feast. The time of its observance depends on the harvest; its purpose is to come together and offer God the first fruits of the harvest; its spirit is one of joyful gratitude for divine blessings. There is also a new theme: seven weeks will separate the first feast of Abib and the feast of the harvest. It seems that this interval had at first no mysterious significance. It was merely a convenient way of determining the time for the assembly at Jerusalem. But it was important enough to justify giving the feast a new name;

thereafter it was called "the feast of Weeks," that is to say, "the feast that follows a week of weeks."

It is surprising that during the Deuteronomist reform the feast remained on an agrarian level (the new name had no doctrinal significance, even though Israel's other great feasts, Passover and Tabernacles—Tents—had moved long before to an historical or even to a moral level. The doctrinal poverty of the feast probably explains the Bible's relative silence in its regard.)

B. THE FEAST OF WEEKS

The first attempt to spiritualize the feast was not made until after the exile and it involves a number symbolism baffling to modern minds. The two new sacerdotal texts attach great importance to the question of the seven weeks:

> Beginning with the day after the Sabbath, the day on which you bring the wave-offering sheaf, you shall count seven full weeks, and then on the day after the seventh week, the fiftieth day, you shall present the new cereal offering to the Lord. For the wave offering of your first fruits to the Lord, you shall bring with you from wherever you live two loaves of bread made of two-tenths of an epha of fine flour and baked with leaven. Besides the bread, you shall offer to the Lord a holocaust of seven unblemished yearling lambs, one young bull, and two rams, along with a sweet-smelling oblation to the Lord. One male goat shall be sacrificed as a sin offering, and two yearling lambs as a peace offering. The priest shall wave the bread of the first fruits and the two lambs as a wave offering before the Lord; these shall be sacred to the Lord and belong to the priest. On this same day you shall by proclamation have a sacred assembly, and no sort of work may be done. This shall be a perpetual

> statute for you and your descendants wherever you dwell. When you reap the harvest of your land, you shall not be so thorough that you reap the field to its very edge, nor shall you glean the stray ears of your grain. These things you shall leave for the poor and the alien (Lev. 23:15-22).

The connection between this feast and the harvest is obvious. The purpose of the celebration was to present the first fruits of the fields to the Lord. The feast's content had not yet changed. But the calculations based on the seven weeks developed and became more important. The newer way of making this calculation was to begin to count the seven weeks, not from the cutting of the first ear, as in Deuteronomy, but from the day after the sabbath that follows this day. Furthermore, it is no longer necessary to count 49 days (that is, seven weeks) but fifty days ($7 \times 7 + 1$). This obviously involves a series of calculations based on the same principles that guided those who invented the perpetual calendar to which reference was made in the chapter on the Passover feast.[34] As a result of these calculations, the feast of Weeks was always celebrated on "the day after the Sabbath." When we speak about Sunday,[35] we will see the doctrinal importance of this reform, which placed an important feast on the day after the Sabbath.

This text and the calculation it proposes occasioned much controversy, especially among those who favored and those who opposed the perpetual calendar. We shall examine first those points on which both sides were in

34 Cf. *supra*, p. 115 ff.
35 Cf. *infra*, p. 173 ff.

agreement, then we shall try to discover the reasons for their disagreement and we shall show how through these disagreements a new and special object was given to the feast of Pentecost.

A first and an important fact to be noted is that according to the calculation in this text there exists a close relationship between Pentecost and the Passover. This solidarity has no great doctrinal depth but it can be said that the feast of Weeks is a satellite of the feast of Passover.

If we look for the foundation of this solidarity we might say that according to the symbolism of numbers, seven times seven days plus one (that is, fifty days) is a sign of plenitude. Later on we shall see that it was calculations like this that explain the origin in the Jewish world of the sabbatical and jubilee year, as well as the prehistory of Sunday (the eighth day). Admittedly at the beginning, the feast of Pentecost was not very important because the content of the feast of the Passover was not sufficiently rich. We shall see that as soon as this meaning deepened, the concept of Pentecostal "fullness" became better understood.

Another important consequence is related to this arithmetical aspect. For a long time the harvest had been the center of interest in the feast; now this shifted to the interval of fifty days following the Passover which Pentecost completed and crowned. The feast of Harvests is "the fiftieth day" or "the Pentecost" which defined and limited a period whose doctrinal content will see many progressive changes.

So much for the points of agreement. As for the points of disagreement, they are based on the different possible ways of solving the mathematical formula. During the first century of our era each Jewish sect had its own method. The Sadducees considered the Passover the first day of the seven weeks. They taught that the word "sabbath" (Lev. 23:15) denoted the day of the feast, which was a day of rest (therefore, "a sabbath"). Pentecost would always fall fifty days after the Passover, no matter what day of the week this would be.

The Pharisees took this prescription of Leviticus literally and began to count their fifty days on the day after the first sabbath after the Passover, that is, the sabbath that fell within the Passover octave. But because they followed the lunar calendar, Pentecost, which always fell on a Sunday, might fall on either of two Sundays, especially if, as happened in the year that Christ died, the Passover fell on a sabbath. The Essenes used this same method, except that they used the perpetual calendar and understood "Passover" to include the whole Paschal week, so the sabbath used as base fell outside the paschal octave. As a result, they often celebrated Pentecost sixty days after the Passover.

During the exchanges of this calendar war, arguments were fashioned by both sides. The Bible was used as an arsenal and this text introducing the promulgation of the Law was often quoted:

> In the third month after their departure from the land of Egypt, on its first day, the Israelites came to the desert of Sinai. . . . Moses went up the mountain to God. Then the Lord called to him and said, "Thus shall you say to the house of Jacob . . ." (Ex. 19:1-4).

This passage was taken to mean that it was on the same day that the Jews departed from Egypt (the fifteenth day of the month), that they arrived at Sinai. This is an obvious allusion to the Essene calculation. Rabbi José ben Halaphta declared in 150 A.D.:

> On the fourteenth Nizan in Egypt the Israelites immolated the Passover lamb; it was a Thursday. . . . In the third month, on the sixth day of the month, the ten commandments; it was a sabbath.[36]

This passage defends the calculation adopted by the Pharisees. But this argument supplies an object for the feast of Pentecost and turns it into a feast of the promulgation of the Law.

Curiously enough, the Essenes adopted the same argument to defend their own calculations. The book of Jubilees, which shows their influence or at least that of Qumran, establishes this in its opening sentence:

> In the third month, on the sixteenth day of the month, Moses ascended the mountain (1:1).

[36] Cf. Strack-Billerbeck, *Kommentar zum N. T.*, II, p. 601. It is a pleasure to thank Dom Jacques Dupont, O.S.B., who allowed me to use the unpublished documentation that he has collected on this subject. See also A. Jaubert, "Le calendrier des Jubilés et de la secte de Qumrân," *Vet. Test.*, 1953, pp. 250-264.

This places Pentecost not fifty days but sixty-one days after the Passover.[37] Despite disagreements about their calculations, the sects did agree to make Pentecost a feast of the promulgation of the Decalogue. Thus only at the beginning of our era did Pentecost receive a new meaning which was not agrarian but historical. It now took its place among the other Jewish feasts which for many years had commemorated the events of the Exodus. Moreover, during the period that the Law was an important subject of meditation of wise men and lawmakers, the two feasts of Passover and Tents were also raised to this same level. It matters little to us that this historical content was achieved in the course of polemics about number calculations and symbolism, and we can proceed to analyze the content.

C. THE FEAST OF THE PROMULGATION OF THE COVENANT

If the two texts that we have just cited, the statement by Rabbi ben Halaphta and the first verse of the book of Jubilees, belong to the last years before our era, it would seem that before Christ's time an effort was made in the Bible to make Pentecost a memorial of the Law. The adoption of a perpetual calendar, of which we have already spoken, made it possible to date a great number of past events, not only in the books that came from priestly

37 Moses' ascent is delayed for a day, no doubt to allow him to observe a day of rest on the feast.

circles (source P and Chronicles) but also in the book of Jubilees.

We have seen that the book of Jubilees placed the promulgation of the Law on Pentecost and it enriched it still more by placing a number of other important biblical events on this same day. The covenant made by God with Noah after the deluge was one of these events:

> God placed His bow in the clouds as a sign of the eternal covenant, whereby there would never again come a deluge to destroy the earth, as long as the earth lasts. For this reason it is prescribed and ordained on the heavenly tablets that the feast of Weeks be celebrated in this month every year, so that the covenant may be renewed every year (6: 16-17).

The author of the book of Jubilees, meditating on the biblical events, also adds to Pentecost the covenant concluded between God and Abraham. The Bible was discreet on this point, giving no definite date (cf. Gen. 15). On the contrary, according to the book of Jubilees, it was on Pentecost, the fifteenth Sivan of the perpetual calendar, that the Lord made a covenant with Abraham (14: 18). The text continues:

> On this day we made a covenant with Abraham just as we did with Noah on this same month. And Abraham renewed the feast and made it a commandment binding forever (14:20).

The rereading of the old documents goes even further. Circumcision, the sign of the Covenant, is observed "during the third month, in the middle of the month" (15:1) and the child of the Covenant, Isaac, is born on the very day of Pentecost (16:3) as the first fruit of the new harvest.

Many other chronological texts could be gleaned from the book of Jubilees, but these suffice to show the growth of the doctrinal content of the feast of the Covenant and various renewals of the Covenant. It is easy to see why it was held in such honor at Qumran, the home of "the covenant community" as it liked to call itself. It seems to have been a kind of patronal feast on which the members renewed the Covenant. Some say that if we compare the beginning of the Qumran community rule with an unedited text of the Damascus Document, we can reconstruct the liturgical rite used in the monastery on Pentecost. During this ceremony the brothers renewed their own covenant and new brothers were introduced into the Covenant.[38]

It is true that none of these documents belong to the canon of sacred scripture. But that does not matter, because in the Bible itself several dates are given for Pentecost that result from the same perspective. Twice the story of Asa's reign is recorded in the Bible. In the book of Kings the royal piety is described (1 Kgs. 15). In the book of Chronicles, written in the second century before Christ and influenced by the perpetual calendar, a long account is given of Asa's reformation, which resembles in the author's eyes the reforms of Josiah and Ezechiel. To crown all Asa's efforts at reform, a large

[38] Milik, *Ten years of discovery in the desert of Judah*, pp. 99-107.

assembly was convoked at Pentecost to renew the Covenant:

> And when they were come to Jerusalem in the third month, in the fifteenth year of the reign of Asa, they sacrificed to the Lord in that day of the spoils, and of the prey, that they had brought, seven hundred oxen, and seven thousand rams. And he went in to confirm as usual the covenant, that they should seek the Lord the God of their fathers with all their heart, and with all their soul. And if anyone, said he, seek not the Lord the God of Israel, let him die, whether little or great, man or woman. And they swore to the Lord with a loud voice with joyful shouting, and with sound of trumpets, and sound of cornets: All that were in Juda with a curse. For with all their heart they swore, and with all their will they sought him, and they found him; and the Lord gave them rest round about (2 Chr. 15:10-15).

This text might seem unimportant if it were not supported by all the texts of the book of Jubilees which show that at this time the feast of Pentecost had become the feast of the promulgation of the Law and had attracted to itself the theme of the renewal of the Covenant.

There is also another reference to the connection of the promulgation of the Law and the feast of Pentecost: the use at an early period of psalm 67 in the Jewish synagogue liturgy on Pentecost. The interpretation given this psalm by the rabbis corroborates this. The psalm praises God's great victories and describes them as the stages of Yahweh's long triumphant procession from Sinai to Sion:

> High the mountains of Basan; rugged the mountains of Basan. Why look you jealously, you rugged mountains, at the mountain God has chosen for his throne, where the Lord himself will dwell forever? The chariots of God are

> myriad, thousands on thousands; the Lord advances from Sinai to the sanctuary. You have ascended on high, taken captives, received men as gifts—even rebels; the Lord God enters his dwelling (Ps. 67:16-19).

Now in the eyes of the rabbis, he who ascended the heights is Moses, who climbed Sinai on the day of Pentecost and who, if he received tribute from men, did so because of the gift of the Law. The rabbis made this a Pentecost psalm and saw in it a hymn of praise for the gift of the Law and the Covenant. Later we shall see how interesting this psalm is in the Pentecost context.

Yet we must never lose sight of the fact that the feast, even though it evolved in this way, had little influence in Israel. Ezechiel's calendar (Ez. 45) does not mention it and biblical references are both few and short (2 Mach. 12:31-32; Tob. 2:1).

Therefore when Christ began His ministry, Pentecost had lost its agrarian character and signified the event of the promulgation of the Law. This required that the faithful make their own the moral attitude of the renewal of the Covenant. This Covenant renewal had once been celebrated in the old feast of Tents, as we have seen.[39] It was then transferred to the Passover when that feast was given a place of primacy in the Jewish calendar. When it was moved to Pentecost, that feast had been associated, at least in the way its date was computed, with the Passover. It shared the soteriological meaning of the Passover and completed its content. The Passover supplied the

39 Cf. *supra*, p. 70 ff.

event, Pentecost showed how life should be lived in the light of the event. The Passover is the independence day of the saved people. Pentecost is the day of the promulgation of their constitution.

D. THE PENTECOST OF THE SPIRIT

On the morning of the Pentecost following the Lord's Passover, the Apostles had assembled, like their contemporaries, to meditate on the promulgation of the Law, no doubt in the light of recent events, when suddenly the phenomena of Sinai were renewed for them:

> And when the days of Pentecost were drawing to a close, they were all together in one place. And suddenly there came a sound from heaven, as of a violent wind blowing, and it filled the whole house where they were sitting. And there appeared to them parted tongues as of fire, which settled upon each of them. And they were all filled with the Holy Spirit and began to speak in foreign tongues, even as the Holy Spirit prompted them to speak (Acts 2:1-4).

All this corresponded to the events of Pentecost on Sinai:

> On the morning of the third day there were peals of thunder and lightning, and a heavy cloud over the mountain, and a very loud trumpet blast, so that all the people in the camp trembled. . . . Mount Sinai was all wrapped in smoke, for the Lord came down upon it in fire (Ex. 19:16-18).

And at the close of the theophany:

> When the people witnessed the thunder and lightening, the trumpet blast and the mountain smoking, they all feared and trembled (Ex. 20:18).

When the rabbis commented on this text, they liked to explain that the people were able to see the flames and hear the voice at the same time because God's voice was in the flame. They often added that this flame was divided into seventy flames to correspond to the seventy peoples of the earth.

It is obvious that the gift of tongues repeats the theme of the promulgation of the Law which was meant to be carried to the ends of the world but which the Jews alone accepted. The promulgation made on the Christian Pentecost will be brought to the four corners of the earth.

This event is the universalist extension of the event of the promulgation of the Law on Sinai.

Psalm 67 also seems to have inspired these events. Peter, apparently, made use of its phrases and especially these verses to explain the mystery of Christ risen and ascended into heaven:

> *Ps:* You have ascended on high (v. 19)
> *Acts:* [David] did not ascend into heaven (2:34)
> *Ps:* you have received . . . (the law, say the rabbis)
> *Acts:* and receiving from the Father the promise of the Holy Spirit (v. 33).[40]

So it seems that Luke, in counting the event produced at Pentecost, was concerned, as was no doubt the whole primitive apostolic tradition, to reread the Sinai event. This feast had become the definitive renewal of the Covenant, a renewal that is not inadequate as were the earlier

[40] It is interesting to note that Ps. 67 is still closely linked with the celebration of the Christian Pentecost liturgy (Introit, etc.).

ones, because this time God, through the gift of the Spirit, will change hearts and minds:

> Behold the days shall come, saith the Lord, and I will make a new covenant with the house of Israel and with the house of Juda: Not according to the covenant which I made with their fathers, in the day that I took them by the hand to bring them out of the land of Egypt: the covenant which they made void, and I had dominion over them, saith the Lord. But this shall be the covenant that I will make with the house of Israel after those days, saith the Lord. I will give my law in their bowels and I will write it in their heart: and I will be their God, and they shall be my people. And they shall teach no more every man his neighbor, and every man his brother, saying: Know the Lord. For all shall know me from the least of them even to the greatest, saith the Lord: for I will forgive their iniquity and I will remember their sin no more (Jer. 31:31-34).

This marks the close of the evolution of the feast of Pentecost in the Bible. After many years this feast was still an agrarian one. As a result of its connection with other feasts it was able to make up for its slow early progress and it commemorated the promulgation of the Covenant. The Passover had been the occasion of the salvation of the Jews and the beginning of their freedom. Pentecost enabled them, by means of the gift of the Law, to preserve their liberty and not to fall back into slavery. Today Easter, the Christian Passover, places Christians within the redemptive event and divine filiation, while Pentecost perfects this work and by means of the gift of the Spirit enables them to realize the ideal of divine filiation and liberations.

E. CONCLUSION

Pentecost, unlike the feasts of the Passover, New Year, and Tents, had no special ritual. The only ceremony prescribed was the offering of the first sheaves of the harvest. When this feast was spiritualized, the renewal of the Covenant became the most important ceremony. Today, as the result of this feast, the Christian is given the power to renew the Covenant. Through God's act the Spirit preserves our bodily life and confirms our liberty. The Law yields place to the Spirit. We no longer are asked to promise anew conformity to an exterior law but to be docile to the inner law of the Spirit (Gal. 5:16). This inner law, like a fire, burns our flesh, and will not be extinguished (1 Thess. 5:19); like wine, it fills and inebriates us (Eph. 5:18); it makes us sons of God and frees us wholly from sin and subjection to exterior law (Gal. 4-5; Rom. 8).

Pentecost, understood in this way, is one with the Passover. On the Passover, Christ the new Adam, received the Spirit of God who raised Him up and made Him Lord and God. We, in our turn, receive this Spirit on Pentecost so that we may live the life of risen men and sons of God. Faith enables us to realize the mystery of this feast.

Chapter Seven

the Sabbath and Sunday

We have examined the feasts of the Jewish liturgy that had astronomical and agrarian origins. Now we wish to analyze the evolution of the Sabbath. While not a feast, strictly speaking, its liturgical importance steadily increased with the years as it left paganism and astrology far behind and became a Christian feast. The Sabbath rest is one element that deserves special attention. It was central in Judaism and continues to raise serious questions in the Christian observance of Sunday. Biblical facts may supply some of these answers. The Sabbath became more than a weekly institution and influenced the sabbatical year and the jubilee year (paralleling Pentecost in terms of years instead of days). So we shall include this system of weeks of years in our survey. Lastly, in creating the Sabbath, the Hebrew religion has shaped the week recognized throughout Christendom.

What is the religious meaning of this division into weeks? What does the week signify in the liturgical cycle? These are the two principal questions we shall try to answer.

A. UNLUCKY DAYS

Sumerian and Babylonian sources disclose regularly recurring unlucky days: the seventh, fourteenth, twenty-first of every month, and the nineteenth (which is the forty-ninth day after the beginning of the preceding month). To do certain things or to undertake certain projects on these days, was to risk divine wrath. Out of fear all work ceased.

The pagan documents we have examined[41] do not indicate that at that time there was anything like a weekly rhythm or a concrete idea of the week. Yet we are justified in seeing in these intervals the distant beginnings of our present week system.[42]

It is probable that the Chosen People observed these days on which, because of fear of the god, no work was done, without any ideas of idolatry or astrology, yet at first they did preserve the note of fear. The Jews rested lest they arouse the wrath of Yahweh.

41 Cf. *supra*, p. 30 ff.

42 By admitting only a remote relation between the Jewish Sabbath and the Babylonian calendar, we acknowledge the difficulties exegetes encounter when they establish a definite connection between the two.

The oldest Jewish explanation of the Sabbath is found in a Yahwist document in which there is an allusion to fear of divine punishment.

> Morning after morning they gathered it, till each had enough to eat; but when the sun grew hot, the manna melted away. On the sixth day they gathered twice as much food, two gomors for each person. When all the leaders of the community came and reported this to Moses, he told them, "That is what the Lord prescribed. Tomorrow is a day of complete rest, the Sabbath, sacred to the Lord. You may either bake or boil the manna, as you please; but whatever is left put away and keep for the morrow." When they put it away for the morrow, as Moses commanded, it did not become rotten or wormy. Moses then said, "Eat it today, for today is the Sabbath of the Lord. On this day you will not find any of it on the ground. On the other six days you can gather it, but on the seventh day, the Sabbath, none of it will be there." Still, on the seventh day some of the people went out to gather it, although they did not find any. Then the Lord said to Moses, "How long will you refuse to keep my commandments and laws? Take note! The Lord has given you the Sabbath. That is why on the sixth day he gives you food for two days. On the seventh day everyone is to stay home and no one is to go out." After that the people rested on the seventh day (Ex. 16:21-30).

This text is basically Yahwistic, even though it does contain priestly corrections. It is based on an exegesis of the word "sabbath" understood as meaning "to abstain" or "to cease." This exegesis is often challenged because it makes "sabbath" a simple modification of "the seventh day."[43] This nuance is relatively unimportant for our research. What emerges is that the Sabbath is a day on which work "ceases" (verses 16, 25, 26, 27), because the

[43] North, "The Derivation of Sabbath," *Bibl.*, 1955, pp. 189-201.

manna ceased. No one can leave camp to find out if there is manna without incurring the risk of God's wrath. This shows that the Sabbath was still, in part, marked by a taboo, but the taboo has now become spiritualized. It was a day consecrated to Yahweh, a "tithing" as it were, of time, just as there was a tithing of the harvest.

Nevertheless, there was a deep change in relation to parallel pagan customs: the Sabbath was related to a desert event. Thus from the beginning it profited from a rethinking of these events in the feasts and days that were part of the Semitic heritage. The taboo has vanished, inasmuch as it is explained in terms not of magic but of history. The Sabbath rest commemorates an event, not a caprice of astrology.

Rest continued to be, even in the rereading of the events of the Exodus, the principal element of the Sabbath; or to correspond more accurately with the mentality of those days, it was a time when work ceased. God required this, else the worker would become the object of divine reprisals. The authors of these narratives had not yet grasped the profound doctrinal reason for this rest.

B. THE DAY OF FREEDOM

Even in the oldest legislative text, the Covenant code, the Sabbath is surrounded with a social mystique surprising for that age, but especially important if we are to understand the evolution of the Sabbath:

> For six days you may do your work, but on the seventh day you must rest, that your ox and your ass may also have rest, and that the son of your maidservant and the alien may be refreshed (Ex. 23:12).

This text, even with its later editing, indicates an extraordinary purification of the Sabbath. No longer is mention made of taboos, or cessation from work out of fear of divine vengeance; the Sabbath is now a day of rest for slaves, strangers, beasts. We may wonder whether this rest has acquired any religious meaning, since its context seems primarily physical and social. At least it brought a sentiment of joy that must have been very real and even at times extravagant, if we are to judge by Osee's statement (2:13) condemning the Sabbath with other gay feasts like lunar observances. But not until the Deuteronomist reform will we find a truly religious reflection on the fact of the physical rest allowed slaves. In fact we read in Deuteronomy:

> Take care to keep holy the Sabbath day as the Lord, your God, commanded you. Six days you may labor and do all your work; but the seventh day is the Sabbath of the Lord, your God. No work may be done then, whether by you, or your son or daughter, or your male or female slave, or your ox or ass or any of your beasts, or the alien who lives with you. Your male and female slaves should rest as you do. For remember that you too were once slaves in Egypt, and the Lord, your God, brought you from there with his strong hand and outstretched arm. That is why the Lord, your God, has commanded you to observe the Sabbath day (Deut. 5:12-15).

This text is particularly important. It establishes rest for every social category, from the head of the Jewish family to the stranger. This is a repetition of the very language of the Covenant code. But this rest is prescribed not so much for the sake of the head of the family, who can do what he wants and rest when he pleases, as for the sake of his inferiors—the servants, beasts, and strangers. The social orientation is obvious. At the time of Deuteronomy an important social evolution was taking place. The small property-owners of the past had been crushed by the urban middle class and found it necessary to rent their services or sell themselves as slaves. The Law took care to ensure these slaves a higher status, and they were given one day of rest each week.

Regulations like this gave rise to the concept of servile work. To be sure, the head of the family and the landowner were forbidden to work, but this prohibition was directed against work which involved their slaves, for whom the day of rest was intended.

This social attitude is characteristic of the general prescriptions of the Law and most especially of the mentality of the Deuteronomist reform, but it is of only secondary religious value. On the other hand, it is most significant that the text we are analyzing gives a religious meaning to the social reform of the Sabbath: "You were once a slave in Egypt and God freed you; do the same with your own slaves and free them one day each week."

We see here a rereading of the legal prescription of physical rest in terms of the historical experience of the desert. Rest is given a new dimension. It is no longer "cessation from work" for its own sake, but it has become a rite to proclaim the liberation of the people from slavery in Egypt. This is why rest referred originally to servile work because it was a better symbol of Egyptian bondage than the occupations of the heads of families or the landowners.

Of all the spiritualizations that the Deuteronomist brought to the liturgy of his day, this seems to be the most significant. The Yahwist document connected the Sabbath rest with a desert event, but in a negative way. The Deuteronomist, on the contrary, catalyzed around rest from servile work the conscience of a people who were proud that they had been freed from Egypt and happy to show this by freeing their subordinates from all work one day each week.

It is precisely on this concept that the prophets will dwell when they wish to obtain a more strict Sabbath observance from the people. A prophet whose work is to be found in the Jeremias collection emphasized this when he insisted on the relation between the Sabbath observance and the future happiness of the people:

> Thus saith the Lord: Take heed to your souls and carry no burdens on the sabbath day: and bring them not in by the gates of Jerusalem. And do not bring burdens out of your houses on the sabbath day: neither do ye any work. Sanctify the sabbath day, as I commanded your fathers. But they did not hear nor incline their ear; but hardened their neck, that they might not hear me and might not receive instruction. And it shall come to pass, if you will hearken to me, saith the Lord, to bring in no burdens by the gates of this city on the sabbath day, and if you will sanctify the sabbath

> day, to do no work therein: Then shall there enter in by the gates of this city kings and princes, sitting upon the throne of David and riding in chariots and on horses, they and their princes, the men of Juda and the inhabitants of Jerusalem: and this city shall be inhabited for ever. And they shall come from the land of Benjamin and from the plains and from the mountains and from the south, bringing holocausts and victims and sacrifices and frankincense: and they shall bring in an offering into the house of the Lord. But if you will not hearken to me, to sanctify the sabbath day, and not to carry burdens, and not to bring them in by the gates of Jerusalem on the sabbath day: I will kindle a fire in the gates thereof. And it shall devour the houses of Jerusalem: and it shall not be quenched (Jer. 17:21-27).

At the moment when this prophecy was edited the inhabitants of Jerusalem had probably been enslaved. The prophet, not without a note of fanaticism, announces the return of freedom and the joyful entry of David's new descendants, provided that they faithfully recognize in the Sabbath the liberty they owe to God's salvation.

C. THE DAY OF IMITATION OF THE LIFE OF GOD

Priestly legislation includes the Sabbath in the complete calendar of the liturgical year as recorded in Numbers 28-29 and Leviticus 23:

> For six days work may be done; but the seventh day is the sabbath rest, a day for sacred assembly, on which you shall do no work. The Sabbath shall belong to the Lord whereever you dwell (Lev. 23:3).
> On the Sabbath day you shall offer two unblemished yearling lambs, with their cereal offering, two tenths of an epha of fine flour mixed with oil, and with their libations. Each

> Sabbath there shall be the Sabbath holocaust in addition to the established holocaust and its libation (Num. 28:9-10).

If we compare these two new prescriptions with all the earlier ones, the difference is fairly obvious. There is still the question of rest, but it now has no social aspect; all levels of society are equally affected. Here cultic elements are stressed:[44] the holy convocation and the nature of the day's sacrifices. Nor is this merely a question of ritual. The priestly documents disclose a basic and highly important theology that sees the Sabbath as the day par excellence on which the Chosen People are privileged to unite themselves to the life of God, to reproduce His ways on their feast day.

The first text containing this new perspective is the priestly account of creation (Gen. 1). This acount is doubtlessly derived from the traditional Babylonian lists of the seven works of the creator-god. The priests, adopting these old tales, sought to show that God the Creator rested from His works on the Sabbath. While the old accounts attributed a special divine work to each day, the priests combined on the third day two distinct works (the separation of sea and land and the creation of plants), so as to leave the last day free and make it a day of rest:

> On the sixth day God finished the work he had been doing. And he rested on the seventh day from all the work he had

[44] Nevertheless an old text must be noted in which the people seem to combine on the Sabbath the teaching and prayer (?) of the schools of the prophets (cf. 2 Kgs. 4:23).

> done. God blessed the seventh day and made it holy because on it he rested from all his work of creation (Gen. 2:2-3).

After reading this story of creation the Jew could conclude that since God had rested on the seventh day, so his own rest was in some way an imitation of the divine rest. So rest was no longer merely the physical rest of the Covenant code or the social rest of Deuteronomy; it is a mode of divine life that man is privileged to enjoy once a week. Hereafter when a legislative text repeats the old prescription of the Covenant code about the Sabbath, this formula is added:

> In six days the Lord made the heavens and the earth, the sea and all that is in them; but on the seventh day he rested. That is why the Lord has blessed the Sabbath day and made it holy (Ex. 20:11).

At the close of a long description of the construction of the sancturary and sacerdotal sanctity (Ex. 25-31), priests added a prescription about the Sabbath that seemed to be irrelevant. Yet a common demoninator in the two texts fully justified the insertion of a law about the Sabbath. Prescriptions regulating the construction of the sancturary, the holy place of God's presence, are followed by prescriptions regulating the vestments of the priest, the sign of God's holiness. So it is not surprising that a reference is made to the Sabbath as the sign of the participation of the people in the holiness of God.

> The Lord said to Moses, "You must also tell the Israelites: Take care to keep my Sabbaths, for that is to be the token between you and me throughout the generations, to show

> that it is I, the Lord, who make you holy. Therefore, you must keep the Sabbath as something sacred. Whoever desecrates it shall be put to death. If anyone does work on that day, he must be rooted out of his people. Six days there are for doing work, but the seventh day is the Sabbath of complete rest, sacred to the Lord. Anyone who does work on the Sabbath day shall be put to death. So shall the Israelites observe the Sabbath, keeping it throughout their generations as a perpetual covenant. Between me and the Israelites it is to be an everlasting token; for in six days the Lord made the heavens and the earth, but on the seventh day he rested at his ease" (Ex. 31:12-17).

So the meaning of the phrase that recurs in the priestly texts, "Yahweh has sanctified the sabbath," and the parallel phrase, "you will sanctify the sabbath," becomes clear. In fact, God has placed in this day a little of His holiness, a little of His mysterious life, and it is the privilege of the Chosen People to be in accord with His holiness at least one day a week.

We should remind ourselves of all that the theme of God's holiness meant at that time. It contained the idea of separation and the idea of the communication of life. The Sabbath recalled this idea of separation from the impure because the Sabbath observance was the "sign" of the Covenant of the Jews with God in the midst of pagan nations. The sanctification of the Sabbath enabled "the saints" to recognize one another.

The Pharisees were not slow in accenting this Sabbath sanctity with detailed rules. Even earlier priestly legislation had introduced certain restrictions—do not light a fire (Ex. 35:3), do not gather wood (Num. 15: 32-36), do not cook food (Ex. 16:23-26)—which were quickly multiplied. For example, reread the interpolation already cited from Jeremias[44] or the reforms initiated by Nehemias:

> In those days, I saw in Juda some treading the presses on the sabbath, and carrying sheaves . . . and bringing them into Jerusalem on the sabbath day. And I charged them that they should sell on a day on which it was lawful to sell. . . . And it came to pass, that when the gates of Jerusalem were at rest on the sabbath day, I spoke. And they shut the gates: and I commanded that they should not open them till after the sabbath. And I set some of my servants at the gate, that none should bring in burdens on the sabbath day (Neh. 13:15-19).

But this was not all. One who did not observe these laws, did not share this holiness, was not a member of this people and should be put to death.

> Whoever desecrates it shall be put to death. If anyone does work on that day, he must be rooted out of his people. . . . Anyone who does work on the Sabbath day shall be put to death (Ex. 31:14-15).
>
> While the Israelites were in the desert, a man was discovered gathering wood on the Sabbath day. Those who caught him at it brought him to Moses and Aaron and the whole assembly. But they kept him in custody, for there was no clear decision as to what should be done with him. Then the Lord said to Moses, "This man shall be put to death; let the whole community stone him outside the camp." So the whole community led him outside the camp and stoned him to death, as the Lord had commanded Moses (Num. 15: 32-36).

It is possible to read betwen the lines of these extremely severe condemnations and to see the high idea that the Jewish people, living after the exile in the midst of pagans, had of their privileges of being the Chosen People

[44] Cf. p. 158-159.

and their intention of defending this privilege at any cost from pagan customs. Beneath this harshness is hidden an admirable insight: the Sabbath is the sign of our membership in the family of God. Not to keep the Sabbath is equivalent to excommunication from the life of the family and the penalty of death is the only logical consequence of this act of treason (cf. Ex. 35:1-3).

Yet we should observe that if the Sabbath increased in importance after the destruction of the temple, it is largely because the great annual feasts of old had lost much of their glory; in fact, they had completely disappeared during the Exile. This doubtlessly explains the proliferation of prohibitions which became increasingly burdensome (Is. 58:13; Jer. 17:21-2; Neh. 13:15-22) and to which the Macchabees gave a strict interpretation (1 Mach. 2:32-41; 2 Mach. 6:11; 15:1-3; 8:25-28).

Yet, it is also possible to cite texts from these years that parallel, as it were, the condemnation texts and promise blessings to those who "keep the sabbath." The idea remains the same: the Sabbath is the rallying point for the rest of the faithful:

> Blessed is the man that doth this, and the son of man that shall lay hold on this: that keepeth the sabbath from profaning it, that keepeth his hands from doing any evil (Is. 56:2).

In answer, no doubt, to an inquiry, it is affirmed in Isaias that the pagan or eunuch who observes the Sabbath is surely included in the Covenant:

For thus saith the Lord to the eunuchs: They that shall keep my sabbaths and shall choose the things that please me and shall hold fast my covenant, I will give to them, in my house and within my walls, a place and a name better than sons and daughters. I will give them an everlasting name which shall never perish (Is. 56:4-6).

It is to be noted that in these two texts the Sabbath obligation has priority over all other moral obligations. The author is merely extending the teaching of Ezechiel that the Sabbath is "the sign between God and His people" and judges the prevarications of their ancestors about their observance of the Sabbath:

And I gave them my statutes, and I shewed them my judgements, which, if a man do, he shall live in them. Moreover, I gave them also my sabbaths, to be a sign between me and them; and that they might know that I am the Lord that sanctify them. But the house of Israel provoked me in the desert: they walked not in my statutes and they cast away my judgements, which if a man do, he shall live in them, and they grievously violated my sabbaths. I said therefore that I would pour out my indignation upon them in the desert and would consume them (Ez. 20:11-13).

It follows that the priestly spiritualization of the Sabbath is very important. The physical repose of the Covenant code or the social rest of Deuteronomy were both human values. The Sabbath rest proposed by the priests had something divine about it; it was a divine initiative, prolonged by man.

The reason for the Sabbath rest is now found in God, and the observance He asks of man is the external sign of the communication of divine life that He offers on the Sabbath. This rest is an invitation to a more-than-natural behavior and worship, the holy assembly, participation in the holiness of worship are sufficient and positive means of sanctifying the Sabbath. The seventh day is no longer an action of man "in honor of Yahweh," but an action of Yahweh, communicated to man, to introduce him into the holiness of God and to separate him from all the other peoples of the earth.

It cannot be denied that Jewish sects, most especially the Pharisees, were fully aware of the greatness of this day and of its importance as a sign of the holiness of God and the Covenant. Unfortunately, the way the Pharisees wished to keep the day holy eventually made it more human than ever because of the meaningless multiplication of prescriptions and exemptions. No one was allowed to carry a bed (Jn. 5:10), care for an invalid (Mk. 3:1-2), or take a walk (Acts 1:12). And the Sabbath that was the sign of a people freed became slavery and an unbearable burden. Christ came into this world of formalistic and detailed regulations. We shall see how He observed the Sabbath and tried, unsuccessfully, to spiritualize it still further.

D. CHRIST AND THE SABBATH

A rapid reading of the gospels shows that most of the arguments between Christ and the Pharisees centered around the observance of the Sabbath. It was also on the Sabbath that He gave some of His most important addresses and preferred to cure and to work miracles.

So it will not be without profit to examine more closely one or another of these episodes in order to discover the spirit of the Jewish Sabbath and observe His conduct. We shall first pause to consider the Lord's reactions as a sign of liberty (a deuteronomical doctrine), so as to isolate, if possible, this characteristic.

If Christ really preferred to work miracles on the Sabbath (cf. Lk. 4, etc.), it is precisely because the Sabbath celebrated the liberation from Egypt and to cure is a way of liberating from evil (hence of celebrating the Sabbath). Luke notes some phrases used by Christ when He was working miracles, that suggest this purpose. Take, for example, the cure of the crippled woman:

> Now he was teaching in one of their synagogues on the Sabbath. And behold, there was a woman who for eighteen years had had a sickness caused by a spirit; and she was bent over and utterly unable to look upwards. When Jesus saw her, he called her to him and said to her, "Woman, thou are *delivered* from thy infirmity." And he laid his hands upon her, and instantly she was made straight, and glorified God. But the ruler of the synagogue, indignant that Jesus had cured on the Sabbath, addressed the crowd saying, "There are six days in which one ought to work; on these therefore come and be cured, and not on the Sabbath." But the Lord answered him and said, "Hypocrites! does not each one of you on the Sabbath *loose* his ox or his ass from the manger, and lead it forth to water? And this woman, daughter of Abraham as she is, whom Satan has bound, lo, for eighteen years, ought not she to be *loosed from this bond* on the Sabbath?" (Lk. 13:10-16).

It does not seem that Christ's vocabulary was chosen by chance. The words "deliver," "loosed from this bond," evoke too closely the liberation which the Sabbath celebrates for us to miss His argument. Since the Sabbath recalls the liberation from Egypt, is it not suitable to celebrate and fulfill it by liberating those held in the chains of Satan's slavery?

The same meaning is to be given to another answer made by the Lord in similar circumstances:

> "I ask you, is it lawful on the Sabbath to do good, or to do evil? to *save* a life, or to destroy it?" (Lk. 6:9).

Another image gives us the same perspective:

> Then addressing them he said, "Which of you shall have an ass or an ox fall into a pit, and will not immediately draw him up on the Sabbath?" (Lk. 14:5).

Christ, who had come to liberate mankind, intended to use the Sabbath as a sign of that liberation. He saw in it the depths of freedom that the Deuteronomist intended it to hold and He intended to preserve this. But the formalism of the Pharisees and the doctors of the law had so burdened the observance of the Sabbath with prescriptions that it was impossible for Christ to manifest His character as liberator in the way He wished.

John expresses the same thought when he speaks of circumcision, which was commonly represented as curing merely the member it directly affected, whereas Christ used this image to show how He cured the whole body:

> For this reason Moses gave you the circumcision—not that it is from Moses, but from the fathers—and on a Sabbath you circumcise a man. If a man receives circumcision on a

> Sabbath, that the Law of Moses may not be broken, are you indignant with me because I made a whole man well on a Sabbath? Judge not by appearances but give just judgment (Jn. 7:22-24).

A second characteristic of the Sabbath is that it is the day of rest par excellence. We have seen how the priests made this rest a divine way of life, a means of emulating the ways of God and manifesting the membership of believing Jews in the family of God. In Christ's arguments with the Jews, He denied this doctrine. The Jews said: "We rest because God rests." Christ denied this after He had once again worked a miracle on the Sabbath:

> And this is why the Jews kept persecuting Jesus, because he did such things on the Sabbath. Jesus, however, answered them, "My Father works even until now, and I work" (Jn. 5:16-17).

God, therefore, does not rest in the negative way taught by the Jews. On the contrary, He never ceases His works of grace and salvation and His Son, to proclaim the family spirit that the Jews sought to manifest by their rest, asserted His solidarity with God by means of His work. Christ's answer makes plain that the Sabbath should be an occasion for sharing in the life of God Himself because it was in this connection that Christ affirmed His divine sonship, which is expressed in the works which He performed and which were not His but His Father's (Jn. 5:19-20). Precisely because the Jewish laws hindered Christ's "work" for the salvation of the world on the Sabbath, He instituted a day on which the latter could be performed—the Sunday of messianic power.

With this thought of sharing in the divine life, the Jews had organized the Sabbath synagogue service in which the Word of Yahweh was proclaimed and explained so that it might mold men's lives. Christ conformed to this law and He frequently attended these services. As any male member could speak on certain occasions, He never failed to proclaim the Good News:

> And he came to Nazareth, where he had been brought up; and according to his custom, he entered the synagogue on the Sabbath and stood up to read. . . . And closing the volume, he gave it back to the attendant and sat down. And the eyes of all in the synagogue were gazing on him. But he began to say to them, "Today this Scripture has been fulfilled in your hearing" (Lk. 4:16-21).

Texts referring to Christ's preaching in the synagogues are many (see Lk. 6:6; 13:10; Jn. 6:60). The Apostles followed His example when they entered a city to preach the Good News, even though this led to their expulsion (Acts. 9:20; 13:5, 14; 17:1-3, 10, 17, etc.).

So we see that Christ wished to fulfill the Sabbath and lift it to a new level of spiritualization. If He opposed the rules for rest and the casuistry that had developed, it was against their human elements that these rules contained and not against the Sabbath itself that He reacted. He only carried to its logical conclusion the theme of liberty and realized the perfection of the Sabbath service in fulfilling the words that had been read there. Unable to achieve this goal, He had to vindicate His messianic function and abrogate the Sabbath. One text is particularly indicative of this spirit:

> At that time Jesus went through the standing grain on the Sabbath; and his disciples being hungry began to pluck ears of grain and to eat. But the Pharisees, when they saw it said to him, "Thy disciples are doing what it is not lawful for them to do on the Sabbath." But he said to them, "Have you not read what David did when he and those with him were hungry? How he entered the house of God, and ate the loaves of proposition which neither he nor those with him could lawfully eat, but only the priests? Or have you not read in the law, that on the Sabbath days the priests in the temple break the Sabbath and are guiltless? But I tell you that one greater than the temple is here. But if you knew what this means, 'I desire mercy, and not sacrifice,' you would never have condemned the innocent; for the Son of Man is Lord even of the Sabbath" (Mt. 12:1-6).

Christ attributes to Himself in this passage two messianic titles to justify His attitude to the Sabbath: *He* is the new temple and the *Lord* of the Sabbath. We must explore the meaning of these titles if we are to understand the transcendence of the Sabbath that they signify.

In presenting Himself as the new temple, Christ meant to give cultic value to the obedience and fraternity that united the Apostles around Him. The cult in the temple which Christ represents is not to be observed by rules and ceremonies conceived by priests and enforced by Pharisees but by an attitude of soul. That is why He applied to Himself the definition of spiritual worship laid down by the prophets: "I desire mercy and not sacrifice."

In this new temple that He established out of obedience to the Father, attitudes of soul and not exterior rubrics constitute true worship. A green field is not defined by the wall of barbed wire that encloses it, but by the grass that grows there. Worship is not defined by ceremonial observances but by the spiritual adherence that it occasions. The Pharisees rendered sterile the progressive spiritualization of the Sabbath by stressing observances over acts of mind and heart.

When Christ declared Himself Lord of the Sabbath, His hearers should have realized that He meant to substitute Himself for Moses and present Himself as a new lawgiver. Not that Moses had failed in his task! This title should be understood in terms of the struggle between Christ and the narrow, fanatical partisans of the Law. The latter had never borne the fruits desired because it was strangled by man-made observances. A new legislator was needed who could organize the Sabbath as He wished.

Moreover, the connection between the Son of Man and the Lord of the Sabbath accounts for Christ's Sabbath role of eschatological judge. Jews of those days expected that the messiah would change the laws, especially the laws governing the Sabbath. For example, this question was proposed to the rabbis: If the messiah were to come, could a Nazirite drink wine on the Sabbath? And the usual answer was that it was the privilege of the messiah to modify ceremonial law.[45]

It was in the midst of such arguments that Christ attempted to spiritualize still further the content of the Sabbath, but formalist objectors made this impossible. Before He could announce an important reform of the

45 Cf. Strack-Billerbeck, *Kommentar zum N.T.*, Vol. II, p. 5.

Sabbath, He was obliged to claim His prerogatives as messiah and head of the new cult.

Christ chose to die at the beginning of the Sabbath (Friday evening) and to spend the whole day of the Great Sabbath in a repose of a new order, death, in order that He might rise the next day. It was a day of dreadful emptiness. It was a day of death. Nothing more can happen . . . "And yet because it was the Passover that was being celebrated and the Jewish sabbath, we must say that it was truly the dead bodies of the Passover and of the sabbath inseparably connected with the body of the crucified that were then celebrated. . . ."[46]

E. THE FIRST DAY OF THE WEEK

If the Lord of the Sabbath chose death on this day, we may ask whether the Old Testament had not prepared the way for the selection of another day more in direct harmony with His plan. It would be an exaggeration to say that the documents of Judaism could have deliberately prepared for the condemnation of a day around which centered so many of its observances. The Sabbath is too much of a pivot for other feasts to be easily supplanted. But at that period number symbolism was held in high esteem, as we had occasion to observe in connection with Pentecost and the perpetual calendar.[47] As a result of these calculations the days of the week benefited, so to

[46] Text of P. Feret in his report to the Congress of Lyons, *Le Jour du Seigneur,* Laffont, 1948.

[47] Cf. *supra,* pp. 115, 138.

speak, each day acquiring a special characteristic, one which was often connected with its number. We shall say more about this below. A special value, however, came to be given to the first day after the Sabbath—Sunday, to give it its Christian name.

Our principal sources of information are the prophets who spoke after the Exile and the book of Jubilees. Supplementary facts may be gleaned from the priestly documents in the Bible.

Let us first review the chronological data supplied by the prophets:

Ezechiel painstakingly dated his visions according to the perpetual calendar. A glance at this calendar[48] suffices to show the prophet's purpose.

His first vision is dated the fifth day of the fourth month (Ez. 1:1), the next occurred on the twelfth day of the same month. Then mention is made of the fifth day of the sixth month (Ez. 8:1), the tenth day of the fifth month (Ez. 20:1), the eleventh day of the tenth month (Ez. 29:1), the first day of the third month (Ez. 31:1), the first day of the twelfth month (Ez. 32:1). If we check these dates on the perpetual calendar we will discover, not without some surprise, that all these visions and oracles took place on a Sunday. It is true that there are some exceptions: two visions occurred on Friday (Ez. 24:1; 40:1) and one on a Wednesday (Ez. 29:17), while two other visions are dated so vaguely that it is impossible to determine the exact day (Ez. 26:1; 32:17).

[48] Cf. *supra*, p. 116.

Yet so many visions took place on Sunday that these exceptions are not noteworthy.

The prophet Zacharias follows Ezechiel closely. One of Zacharias' two visions took place on a Sunday (Zach. 1:7), while the vision of Aggeus the prophet also occurred on a Sunday (Aggeus 1:1).

If we turn from prophetic to priestly sources, we see that when dates are given for events, they rarely fall on Sunday, more frequently on Wednesday and Friday.[49] Yet two events do occur on Sunday and they are precisely two apparitions of God: the first is at the beginning of creation (Gen. 1:3-5), the second is the apparition of God to Noah on the day of the deluge (Gen. 7:11).

Does this mean that Sunday is the day set apart for God's apparitions in the world and God's visions to the prophets? The book of Jubilees points to this conclusion. There is use and abuse of the dates of events and nothing is omitted, but it is curious to note that the chief apparitions of God occur on Sunday. God spoke to Abraham on the first day of the third month (Jub. 14:1) and returns to speak to him again on the fifteenth day of the same month (Jub. 15:1). God's miraculous initiative assuring Isaac's conception likewise took place on Sunday (Jub. 16:12).[50]

Does there not seem to be here the beginning of a mystique of Sunday, in virtue of which Sunday is the day

49 Cf. *infra*, pp. 193-195.

50 Most of these references are taken from Mlle. Jaubert's book cited above. Yet she makes no effort to point out the specific nature of Sunday in these texts.

par excellence for divine initiatives and appearances, the day above all others when the prophets touch eternal secrets and eschatological visions?

If Christ wished to find a day other than the Sabbath to exercise the fullness of the Sabbath realities, as we have seen in connection with the feast of the Passover on the perpetual calendar, does it not seem likely that he would choose the first day of the week for the exercise of His prerogatives?

F. THE DAY OF APPARITIONS

Throughout His public life Christ did not attach the least importance to the first day of the week and the Evangelists record no episode that fell on that day and that could help us to shape its theology. Until His death, Christ faithfully observed the Sabbath, even though He tried ceaselessly to lift its observance to a new and higher spiritual level. Only after His death and throughout the last weeks of His risen life in the midst of His Apostles did He clearly manifest His intention of establishing Sunday as a new day of worship.

For the moment we shall limit ourselves to an examination of the different episodes that manifest this will. Then we shall analyze in more detail the content of each text.

On the first Sunday after His passion, Christ appeared several times, the first time to Mary Magdalene:

> But Mary was standing outside weeping at the tomb. So, as she wept, she stooped down and looked into the tomb, and saw two angels in white sitting, one at the head and one at the feet, where the body of Jesus had been laid. They said to her, "Woman, why art thou weeping?" She said to them, "Because they have taken away my Lord, and I do not know where they have laid him." When she had said this she turned around and beheld Jesus standing there, and she did not know that it was Jesus. Jesus said to her, "Woman, why art thou weeping? Whom dost thou seek?" She, thinking that he was the gardener, said to him, "Sir, if thou hast removed him, tell me where thou hast laid him and I will take him away." Jesus said to her, "Mary!" Turning, she said to him, "Rabboni!" (that is to say, Master). Jesus said to her, "Do not touch me, for I have not yet ascended to my Father, but go to my brethren and say to them, 'I ascend to my Father and your Father, to my God and your God' " (Jn. 20:11-18).

A few hours later He appeared to Peter, no doubt to show by this choice Peter's priority over the other Apostles (Lk. 24:34).

Late that afternoon the Lord appeared to the disciples at Emmaus.

> And it came to pass, while they were conversing and arguing together, that Jesus himself also drew near and went along with them; but their eyes were held, that they should not recognize him. . . . And they drew near to the village to which they were going. . . . And he went in with them. And it came to pass when he reclined at table with them, that he took the bread and blessed and broke and began handing it to them. And their eyes were opened, and they recognized him; and he vanished from their sight. And they said to each other, "Was not our heart burning within us while he was speaking on the road and explaining to us the Scriptures? . . . And they themselves began to relate what had happened on the journey, and how they recognized him in the breaking of the bread (Lk. 24:15-16, 28, 30-32, 35).

Finally, fairly late in the evening of that same day, the Lord appeared for the fourth time:

> When it was late that same day, the first of the week, though the doors where the disciples gathered had been closed for fear of the Jews, Jesus came and stood in the midst and said to them, "Peace be to you!" . . . "As the Father has sent me, I also send you." When he had said this, he breathed upon them, and said to them, "Receive the Holy Spirit; whose sins you shall forgive, they are forgiven them; and whose sins you shall retain, they are retained" (Jn. 20:19-23).

On the following Sunday there is another apparition:

> And after eight days, his disciples were again inside, and Thomas with them. Jesus came, the doors being closed, and stood in their midst (Jn. 20:26).

It was probably on one of the later Sundays that another apparition occurred. The Apostles had spent an entire day together doing nothing, which suggests that it was the Sabbath. When evening came and the Sabbath was over, Peter got up and went to work. Some of the disciples followed him. They worked all night, and the next morning, that is Sunday morning, the following incident took place:

> But when the day was breaking, Jesus stood on the beach; yet the disciples did not know that it was Jesus. Then Jesus said to them, "Young men, have you any fish?" They answered him, "No." He said to them, "Cast the net to the right of the boat and you will find them." They cast therefore, and now they were unable to draw it up for the great number of fishes. . . . When, therefore, they had breakfasted, Jesus said to Simon Peter, "Simon, son of John, dost thou love me more than these do?" He said to him, "Yes,

Lord, thou knowest that I love thee." He said to him, "Feed my sheep" (Jn. 21:4-17).

According to an old tradition it was on a Sunday that the Lord appeared to His Apostles for the last time and then ascended into heaven. The epistle of the Pseudo-Barnabas, in speaking of Sunday, says:

It was on this day that the Christ rose from the dead and ascended into the heavens after His apparitions (15:9).

This tradition is reported by other eastern authors.[51] It must be admitted that this is not contrary to the facts as reported in Scripture. If the book of Acts states that the Lord remained forty days with His disciples, forty is a number so richly symbolic that it need not be taken too literally. Moreover, the author of Acts, in finishing his gospel, places the Ascension in perfect continuity with the apparition of Easter Sunday:

Now he led them out towards Bethany, and he lifted up his hands and blessed them. And it came to pass as he blessed them, that he parted from them and was carried up into heaven. And they worshipped him, and returned to Jerusalem with great joy. And they were continually in the temple, praising and blessing God (Lk. 24:50-54).

The tradition reproduced by the Pseudo-Barnabas is doubtlessly derived from the Lukan text. But these words were meant merely to be a description of the Lord's disappearance after one of His apparitions, and were not intended to be a description of the definitive Ascension. Whatever may be the answer to this question,

51 For example, Addai's *Didascalia*.

happily other texts are clearer. It was also on a Sunday—the Sunday of Pentecost—that the Spirit of the Lord appeared under the form of tongues of fire. We will quote the text to which we have already alluded, because its content will help us to discover the theology of Sunday:

> And when the days of Pentecost were drawing to a close, they were all together in one place. And suddenly there came a sound from heaven, as of a violent wind blowing, and it filled the whole house where they were sitting. And there appeared to them parted tongues as of fire, which settled upon each of them. And they were all filled with the Holy Spirit . . . (Acts 2:1-4).

As to the last apparition of the Lord which the New Testament dates, it too occurred on a Sunday. This is the apparition of the glorified Christ to the author of the Apocalypse:

> I, John, your brother and partner in the tribulation and kingdom and patience that are in Jesus, was on the island which is called Patmos, because of the word of God and the testimony of Jesus. I was in the spirit on the Lord's day, and I heard behind me a great voice, as of a trumpet, saying, "What thou seest write in a book" . . . (Apoc. 1:9-11).

Of course all of Christ's undated apparitions to His disciples cannot possibly be assigned to Sundays: the apparition to the five hundred (1 Cor. 15:6), the apparition to James, the head of the Jewish community (1 Cor. 15:7) and an apparition to the Apostles (Acts 1:3) which probably coincides with one of the apparitions that we described above. So it is evident that, with these few exceptions, primitive Christian tradition looked on Sunday as the normal day for the Lord to appear, just as in the Old Testament it had been the normal day for God to appear to the prophets. To show that Christ was continuing Yahweh's prophetic apparitions is one way of saying that He is Lord and God.

To the first Christians Sunday was therefore the day when the Lord was still in their midst. But there is a vast difference between the Jewish Sabbath and the Christian Sunday. The latter was in no way like days held sacred in all religions, or like the Sabbath, a day consecrated and sanctified by man in honor of God. On the contrary, it was a day on which the Lord chose to appear. Admittedly the Jews had taken the first steps towards this concept when they based the Sabbath on God's historic initiative, but they soon filled the day with human observances and considerably diminished its theological dimension. For Christians, on the contrary, the Lord's manifestations are central to and inseparable from the meaning of Sunday. In God and not in man is to be found the final reason for Sunday.

G. THE LORD'S DAY

Although New Testament documents usually refer to Sunday by its Jewish name, calling it "the first day of the week," or "the first day after the sabbath," in one document the content of this day has been rethought and its specifically Christian meaning weighed so that Sunday is given a new name, "the day of the Lord" (Apoc.

1:10). To be perfectly faithful to the author's thought, we should call it the *Dies Domini,* the "dominical day." In fact, the "day of the Lord" was too closely connected in Jewish thought with "the day of Yahweh," with all its concomitant cataclysms and judgments. In introducing "the Lord's day," the author of the Apocalypse, without completely ignoring Sunday's eschatological dimension, prefers to stress its present relationship to Christ and His mysterious presence and messianic powers.

Now it is precisely this aspect of the presence of the risen Christ in the midst of this new people that is stressed in the apparition accounts. To us it seems interesting to point out that in most of these apparitions Christ did not allow Himself to be recognized immediately on the physical plane: Mary Magdalene mistook Him for the gardener; the disciples for a traveler; the fishermen on the lake did not dare to press too far the question of His identity; Thomas doubted until he placed his fingers in the wounds; when He was in their midst, the band of Apostles discussed the restoration of the earthly kingdom, etc. If Christ refused His followers all physical experience of Himself, if He even went so far as to repel Mary Magdalene with the words, "Do not touch Me," yet He took care to substitute for the physical experience of His presence, another and mysterious type of experience. In this way at Emmaus when He was with the disciples who did not recognize Him, He first explained to them the Scriptures, then He divided the loaf and "they knew Him in the breaking of bread." He made it possible for the fishermen on the lake, who were hesitating about His identity, to draw in a miraculous catch and thus fulfill the messianic prophecy of Ezechiel (Ez. 47); only then were they able to recognize Him in the power He had given them. On Easter Sunday evening the apostles who were terrified when He appeared in their midst, heard Him confer upon them the power of pardoning sin, which the Jews had always believed to be one of the fundamental messianic powers.

Thus the Apostles learned that Sunday has a double dimension: it is the day on which the messianic powers of the end of time are made manifest, and it is also a day which indicates that the end-time has already begun.

Thomas was failing in faith when he continued to ask for a physical experience of the Lord's presence, who is now to be found in another mode of presence. He is to be found in the exercise of the powers He gave His followers: in baptism, mission assignments, the forgiveness of sin,[52] the Eucharist, etc.

So, on one day each week—Sunday—the Christians enjoyed the fullness of the messianic powers which were to be distributed with great liberality for all eternity until the Lord would come again. Sunday was, as it were, an anticipation of eternal life. The New Testament, we must admit, does not insist on this point but the early Church stressed it and gave Sunday a new name, calling it "the

52 See p. 206 for the meaning of the forgiveness of sins in conjunction with the Jubilee Year.

eighth day." We cannot refrain from citing in this connection the beautiful text of the *Didascalia* of Addai:

> The apostles decided that on Sunday would be office, the reading of the holy books and the offering of the eucharist, because it was on a Sunday that Christ rose from the dead, rose into heaven, and it will be again on a Sunday that He will appear to us at the end accompanied by His angels.

One text has special meaning in this regard. It consists of a warning found in the Epistle to the Hebrews:

> Not forsaking our assembly as is the custom of some, but exhorting one another, and this all the more as you see the Day drawing near (Heb. 10:25).

In conclusion, let us point out that the Church remained faithful to the Lord's work, since it is correct to say that Sunday was instituted by Him. It was on a Sunday that He sent the Apostles on their mission. It was on a Sunday that the Church consecrated bishops and ordained priests. It was on a Sunday that He was recognized in the breaking of bread. It was on Sundays that the Church required bishops to preach and offer the liturgy of the Word. There are many ancient prescriptions that continue this parallel.

H. THE DAY OF THE ASSEMBLY

If we reread the accounts of Christ's apparitions, we will see that most of them state, not without a certain insistence, that the Apostles were all assembled together in one place.

> Where they found the Eleven gathered together and those who were with them (Lk. 24:33).
> When it was late that same day, the first of the week, though the doors where the disciples assembled had been closed[53] (Jn. 20:19).
> And after eight days, his disciples were again inside (Jn. 20:26).
> They therefore who had come together (Acts 1:6).
> They were all together in one place (Acts 2:1).
> And on the first day of the week, when we had met for the breaking of bread (Acts 20:7).

John notes that each apparition occurred during a reunion of the Apostles and Luke goes further and describes this union as an assembly. It seems likely that there is a good reason why this theme reappears so often in the account of these apparitions and it is not difficult to grasp the authors' purpose.

The term "assembly" (*qahal* in Hebrew, *ecclésia* in the Septuagint) is found in Deuteronomist documents to denote the assembly convoked by Yahweh at Sinai to seal the Covenant:

> Assemble the people for me; I will have them hear my words, that they may learn to fear me as long as they live in the land and may so teach their children (Deut. 4:10).

But it seems likely that there is in this text a projection of the desert event into the official assemblies of the people in Jerusalem that the Deuteronomist organized around the three important feasts of the year:

53 The word "assembled" was probably added later to this context, but this addition has value because it reveals the concern of primitive tradition to recognize the assembly of the Apostles as the prelude of the Sunday assembly.

> Three times a year, then, every male among you shall appear before the Lord, your God, in the place which he chooses: at the feast of Unleavened Bread, at the feast of Weeks, and at the feast of Booths (Deut. 16:16).

As a matter of fact the people's great liturgical feasts were frequently the occasion of particularly solemn assemblies in which the people renewed their own commitment and the divine election (2 Kgs. 23; Neh. 8:17; 13:1). But this assembly formula was not definitive, nor its meaning fully clarified. So the prophets projected into the future the ideal assembly in which not only the tribes of Israel but all the nations would come together:

> And the Gentiles shall walk in thy light, and kings in the brightness of thy rising.
> Lift up thy eyes round about and see: all these are gathered together, they are come to thee (Is. 60:34).

When Luke and John made their own the assembly mystique, they wished to signify that this assembly is now realized in the Sunday reunion of the disciples about the Lord who is mysteriously present in their midst.

Several consequences follow.

First of all, the presciption requiring the presence of the people in Jerusalem for each of the great feasts was replaced by the prescription that they meet every Sunday. Sunday alone became the heir of all the Jewish feasts. It was given pre-eminence over any Jewish feasts that were later introduced into the Christian calendar. Historically, it cannot be proved that there is any continuity between the Jewish Passover and the Christian feast of Easter or between the Jewish Pentecost and the Christian Pentecost, while it is certain that Sunday has been celebrated as a feast day since the last weeks of Christ's risen life.

Moreover, it is significant that all Christian Churches have always agreed unanimously about Sunday observance and less than unanimously about the observance of Easter and other feasts. This allows us to suppose that Sunday enjoyed a certain pre-eminence, at least in the logical order, over other feasts. In this connection it is well to note that the paschal quarrels were settled in the Church by the decision to celebrate Easter, not on its exact anniversary, but always on the *Sunday* following the anniversary. In other words, the Sunday aspect was given priority over the historical aspect.

Sunday, therefore, is the day of the official assembly of the people, of the assembly that makes them a people by divine convocation in terms of the powers of the Son (cf. Acts 20:7). It is the day on which the Church becomes aware of itself and of what characterizes it as itself. Consequently, the Apostles saw clearly the paramount importance of this assembly which is a visible sign of the unity of the Church in the midst of a disordered and disunited world:

> For first of all I hear that when you meet in church there are divisions among you, and in part I believe it. . . . So then when you meet together, it is no longer possible to eat the Lord's Supper . . . (1 Cor. 11:17-20).
>
> When you come together each of you has a hymn, has an instruction, has a revelation, has a tongue, has an interpretation. Let all things be done unto edification (1 Cor. 14: 26-27).

The insight that in the unity of the assembly, one participates more perfectly in the reality that is the Church, is also shown in the way Paul asked that the collection be made for the poor of Jerusalem. He might merely have proposed that money be set aside and promised that when he arrived he would take it with him, but he wished to make this offering sacral and to give it an ecclesial dimension, so he fixed a date for this collection and gave an official setting to an otherwise absolutely private act:

> Now concerning the collection being made for the saints, as I have ordered the churches of Galatia, do you also. On the first day of the week, let each one of you put aside at home and lay up whatever he has a mind to, so that the collections may not have to be made after I have come. (1 Cor. 16:1-2).

In this way the day of assembly, Sunday, became a day of special charity. Eventually the Sunday assembly became obligatory, and we should not lose sight of the fact that the reason for this obligation was above all because it was an image of the Church in act. Spread out day by day in the individual work of each of its members, the kingdom of God is restored every Sunday in the unity of the Body of Christ. It is sad that some are absent:

> Let us not forsake our own assembly, as some are in the habit of doing . . . (Heb. 10:25).

A beautiful text from the Eastern tradition will serve as conclusion to this point:

> When you teach, command and persuade the people to be faithful to assemble in Church. May they not fail to do this

but may they faithfully meet together so that no one will diminish the Church by his absence nor separate a single member from the Church. May no one apply the Lord's words only to his neighbors: "He who does not gather with Me, scatters." Because you are Christ's members, do not lose yourselves outside the Church by not coming to its assemblies. . . . Do not despise yourselves by dismembering the Body of Christ.[54]

I. CONCLUSION

Why did Sunday replace the Sabbath? This seems to be the question we should ask ourselves at the close of this rapid scriptural survey.

Between the Jewish Sabbath and the Christian Sunday there is above all the mystery of the Lord's death and resurrection. We have seen that Christ involved the institution of the Sabbath in His own death so that He might institute the Christian Sunday. This is a fundamental law of the evolution and Christianization of human feasts and even of Jewish feasts—first, there must be a death to their first meaning and content, so that there can be a new life in which they continue to be themselves in a new form and in a more spiritual context. The Christian axiom: "Man must be reborn to a new life," is true also of feasts.

If we consider, for example, the repose so characteristic of the Jewish Sabbath, we will find that it is not an essential element of Sunday observance. Christ met the repose of death and if repose is part of our observance, it is His gift, not that of the Sabbath:

54 *Didascalie des apôtres,* chap. 13, Ed Nau, p. 116 (3rd century).

> Let us receive according to the spirit and practice according to the spirit, all that is written about the sabbath. Thus should we understand the sabbath rest. But now there is but one sabbath: we possess it in Jesus Christ, our redeemer (Greogry the Great, Letter 63).

Christ, in fact, declared that He and His Father "work" on the Sabbath, just as they work on other days. If we are to rest on our Sabbath it is in order that we may unite ourselves to the work of God's grace and salvation in us. Rest has no absolute value. It serves merely to free us from work that is too human so that we may take part in work that is God's; so that we may share in the messianic powers He has confided to His Son and to which we have access in the Christian assembly.

Even in the old dispensation the Sabbath denoted a time of liberation from servile work. It was a sign of the freedom of a people no longer in bondage. But why celebrate the escape from Egyptian servitude, if one has been pressed into the bondage of an external and formal observance? Is not Sunday the true sign of liberation because it denotes Christ's victory over servile work as well as over the slavery of sin and death?

How better can we express our freedom? Negatively by merely abstaining from servile work? Or by abstaining from sin? If Christ, appearing to His Apostles for the first time on Easter Sunday, conferred upon them the power to forgive sin, is it not an invitation to make Sunday a sinless day, a day most closely linked with the Messiah's power over Satan? Do we not often slip into a Sabbath frame of mind when we draw fine distinctions about the kind of work allowed on Sundays, when we define and re-define servile work to separate it from non-servile work, totally unmindful that the latter may often hold us in servitude to money or passion when manual work may be performed as simple relaxation or to prevent idleness?

Sunday continues, therefore, like the Sabbath, to be a day of liberty and liberation, but Christ invites men of every social category to enjoy this liberation which is a victory over sin and a triumph over death.

The Jewish Sabbath united the whole family in a common act of faith. Servants and maids, strangers and even cattle had a part in this feast, at least inasmuch as all shared a common equality in the sight of God. The resonances of the Sabbath were all of love. But it was a charity that went no further than the walls of the home. The Lord changed this. In His Sunday apparitions, He bade His disciples to go out into the whole world and thus gave the dimensions of the whole Church to the Sunday assembly. It continued to be a family gathering and one marked by charity, but because of the openness of its spirit it was now cosmic. Moveover, recurring periodically as it does, it constitutes an official people, a royal people, a holy priesthood who thereby became more and more perfectly aware of their unity and meaning.

Lastly, the Jewish Sabbath was turned to the past. True, it commemorated a present state of liberty but a liberty acquired long ago. Sunday, on the contrary, if it celebrates the possession here and now of Christian liberty, is totally orientated towards the "Day of the Lord" on which Christ will come again. Sunday recapitulates all other Jewish feasts. All of these feasts lead toward Sunday and the only ones among them that preserve a certain autonomy in the Church are precisely the two that are observed on a Sunday: Easter and Pentecost. Submerged as we are today in a calendar overcrowded with feasts, it is easy for us to lose sight of Sunday's special place. No other exterior solemnity can make a feast more important than Sunday. No feast, no day of devotion, will ever enjoy the distinction of being the official assembly of God's people nor will it embrace so many messianic graces.

Chapter Eight

Wednesday and Friday

We have referred to the pattern of the week in our study of the Sabbath and Sunday; let us now see what Scripture has to say about the other days of the week. Have they any cultic value? Any religious meaning?

Sunday became, in the perpetual calendar, the Christian day par excellence. What special modality do the other days of the perpetual calendar enjoy?

A. WEDNESDAY

According to Mlle. Jaubert (whose work we have frequently quoted), all the events that are dated in the priestly documents of the Pentateuch fall on a Sunday or a Wednesday or a Friday.

Among the events that took place on a Wednesday may be noted: the appearance of the first mountain peaks as the waters of the deluge began to subside (Gen. 8:5); the appearance of dry land when the waters had completely subsided (Gen. 8:13-15); the departure from Egypt (Ex. 12:31-51; Num. 33:3); the erection of the tabernacle in the desert (Ex. 40:1-17); the departure from Sinai (Num. 20:1); the departure from Babylon (Esd. 7:9); the opening of Esdras' court (Esd. 10:16); the close of the final session of his court (Esd. 10:17); the assembly of the new people (Neh. 8:12); Ezechiel's oracle against Egypt (Ez. 29:17); Zacharias's fasting oracle (Zach. 7:1); the beginning of Nabuchodonosor's campaign (Jud. 2:1); the first day of the temple restoration ceremonies (1 Mach. 4:52); the inscription on the tablets of bronze (1 Mach. 14:27); the departure of Adam and Eve from Paradise (Jubilees 3:32); the celebration of their first feast (Jubilees 7:2); the apparition of angels to Abraham (Jubilees 16:1); the birth of Levi, Joseph, etc.

All this may seem at first quite fortuitous. Yet a meaning emerges when we recall that with only one exception (Ez. 30:20), Wednesday and Friday are the only weekdays recognized in the Bible. Obviously Wednesday enjoyed a special place in the Jewish week. Can this thought be developed further? First of all, there is the New Year Wednesday (the first day of the seventh month or the first day of the first month). According to Nehemias (8:2) and Jubilees (7:2), this was the usual day for the feast. The perpetual calendar was structured so that the year would always begin on a Wednesday and the quarterly new moons would always fall on the same day. In fact, it was on a Wednesday that the heavenly bodies were created (Gen. 1:14-19), so it follows that the year which is subject to their revolution should also begin on that day.

For this reason many events were planned so as to begin on a Wednesday: the departure from Egypt and from Babylon were arranged to begin on that day; the Passover, according to the perpetual calendar, always fell on a Wednesday. Those events that are recorded as taking place on a Wednesday often have some aspect of a paschal liberation. Besides the departures from Egypt and Babylon, which are intentionally parallel, we should recall that the liberation from the waters of the Deluge began on a Wednesday but took place in several stages: the waters began to diminish (Gen. 8:3), mountain peaks appeared (Gen. 8:5), the waters dried (Gen. 8:13), the dry land appeared (Gen. 8:14). In the same way, most of the great stages of the liberation from Egypt and the journey through the desert occurred on a Wednesday: the departure from Sinai, the construction of the tabernacle, etc.

Wednesday, therefore, is the sign of the beginning of a year or of a new era and also of a departure. At the same time it is a sign of liberation which is understood in terms of a setting out on a fresh start.

B. FRIDAY

If we examine events assigned to a Friday, we will see that they are frequently connected with arrivals. Because a Jew could not travel on a Saturday, his travels were expected to end on a Friday!

So we find that it was on a Friday that the Ark reached Mount Ararat (Gen. 8:4), and the people reached the Promised Land (Jos. 4:19). Likewise, after the departure from Babylon, as if the better to recall the Exodus, it was also on Friday that the exiles returned to Palestine. This joy was not unalloyed and it was on a Friday that Nabuchodonoser besieged Jerusalem (4 Kgs. 25:1).

If Friday is the day for arrivals and the bringing of men to their desired goals, it is also an appropriate day for death. It was on a Friday that Aaron died (Num. 33:38).

Lastly, it is a day for expiation. On Friday the paschal lamb was chosen (Ex. 12:3). On Friday (the tenth day of the seventh month) the feast of Expiation was celebrated, and it was sometimes a day of penance (Neh. 9:1).

The Jews, we have seen, had a somewhat symbolic conception of the days of the week, especially Wednesday and Friday. Does this point to a mystique of numbers? This is possible, especially for Wednesday and the number 4. It seems less likely for Monday and Thursday, which are sometimes referred to as days of fast.

Curiously, Scripture records no event taking place on a Tuesday.

Chapter Nine

the Sabbatical Year and the Jubilee

Our study of the Sabbath would not be complete if we failed to allude to the sabbatical year and the jubilee year, which are in a cycle of seven years as the Sabbath is in a cycle of seven days. Only a brief allusion need be made to many of the elements because in both cycles they are the same.

A. THE SABBATICAL YEAR

The observance of the sabbatical year was based on a widespread and sensible agrarian custom of early times. To ensure good crops the soil was left fallow from time to time. The soil of Palestine was not nearly as rich as that of Egypt which was annually fertilized by the Nile, therefore, the law forbade the uninterrupted cultivation of the soil.

The Hebrews adopted this rule as soon as they entered the Promised Land, and the Covenant code is the oldest legislative text that treats this subject. But from the beginning the agrarian level was transcended and, like the Sabbath rest, the institution became part of the social order:

> For six years you may sow your land and gather in its produce. But the seventh year you shall let the land lie untilled and unharvested, that the poor among you may eat of it and the beasts of the field may eat what the poor leave. So also shall you do in regard to your vineyard and your olive grove. For six days you may do your work, but on the seventh day you must rest, and the son of your maidservant, and the alien may be refreshed (Ex. 23:10-12).

Thus Moses immediately situated the institution on a charitable and social plan without, however, infringing on good farming practice. Note the parallelism that exists between laws governing the Sabbath and jubilee year. One spirit animates both. We shall see that this is true of the whole evolution of the sabbatical year.

Even in the Covenant code the charitable aspects of the sabbatical year are stressed:

> When you purchase a Hebrew slave, he is to serve you for six years, but in the seventh year he shall be given his freedom without cost. If he comes into service alone, he shall leave alone; if he comes with a wife, his wife shall leave with him. But if his master gives him a wife and she bears

> him sons or daughters, the woman and her children shall remain the master's property, and the man shall leave alone. If, however, the slave declares, 'I am devoted to my master and my wife and children; I will not go free,' his master shall bring him to God and there, at the door or doorpost, he shall pierce his ear with an awl, thus keeping him as his slave forever (Ex. 21:2-6).

The text is ambiguous. It is difficult to know whether all slaves were liberated during the seventh calendar year, that is, during the official jubilee year (this seems unlikely), or during their seventh year of service. There is evidence that this liberation was later connected with the jubilee year. The price of a Hebrew slave depended, therefore, on the number of years that would elapse until the next sabbatical year. Note, too, that this prescription was not inspired by strictly religious considerations. It was intended merely to preserve Hebrews from too long a period of servitude and too preserve the members of a powerful and free people from permanent enslavement. Humane as this concept surely is, it is also singularly charitable and supposes a highly developed understanding of the liberty of a people and of the close union of its members.

In this legislation we see once again the same concept of the liberation of slaves that we noted in our study of the Sabbath. The Hebrew slave was a member of a free people; every sabbath, therefore, he should enjoy his freedom, and recover it definitely every seven years.[55] But with the extension of urban civilization during the king-

55 See *supra,* p. 155.

dom, some serious social changes followed, and they could not be solved by the traditional laws of fallow fields and the liberation of slaves at stated times. As the cities grew in size, lands were alienated and small, landed proprietors could live only if they placed themselves under the patronage of a rich, middle-class city man. Many biblical texts allude to the economic unrest of this period and to the exploitation of the poor by the rich:

> And after these times, Naboth the Jezrahelite, who was in Jezrahel, had at that time a vineyard near the palace of Achab king of Samaria.
> And Achab spoke to Naboth, saying: Give me thy vineyard, that I may make me a garden of herbs, because it is nigh, and adjoining to my house: and I will give thee for it a better vineyard. Or if thou think it more convenient for thee, I will give thee the worth of it in money. Naboth answered him: The Lord be merciful to me and not let me give thee the inheritance of my fathers (3 Kgs. 21:1-3).

Naboth's fate is well known. He is the peasant who would become one of the proletariat if he yielded to the pressures exerted by the rich, and he would be reduced to death if he resisted. The prophets of those days did not speak gently when they addressed the rich who "join house to house, who connect field with field . . . until no room remains and they are left to dwell alone in the midst of the land" (Is. 5:8).

Laws enacted in Deuteronomist circles were designed to meet this new situation and force the rich, during the sabbatical year, to restore to the peasants the lands they had seized either as pledges or as payment of debts contracted during the previous six years:

> At the end of every seven-year period, you shall have a relaxation of debts, which shall be observed as follows. Every creditor shall relax his claim on what he has loaned his neighbor; he must not press his neighbor, his kinsman, because a relaxation in honor of the Lord has been proclaimed. You may press a foreigner, but you shall relax the claim on your kinsman for what is yours. Nay, more! since the Lord, your God, will bless you abundantly in the land he will give you to occupy as your heritage, there should be no one of you in need. If you but heed the voice of the Lord, your God, and carefully observe all these commandments which I enjoin on you today, you will lend to many nations and borrow from none; you will rule over many nations, and none will rule over you, since the Lord, your God, will bless you as he promised. If one of your kinsmen in any community is in need in the land which the Lord, your God, is giving you, you shall not harden your heart nor close your hand to him in his need. Instead, you shall open your hand to him and freely lend him enough to meet his need. Be on your guard lest, entertaining the mean thought that the seventh year, the year of relaxation, is near, you grudge your help to your needy kinsman and give him nothing: else he will cry to the Lord against you and you will be held guilty. When you give to him, give freely and not with ill will; for the Lord, your God, will bless you for this in all your works and undertakings. The needy will never be lacking in the land; that is why I command you to open your hand to your poor and needy kinsman in your country. If your kinsman, a Hebrew man or woman, sells himself to you, he is to serve you for six years, but in the seventh year you shall dismiss him from your service, a free man. When you do so, you shall not send him away empty-handed, but shall weigh him down with gifts from your flock and threshing floor and wine press, in proportion to the blessing the Lord, your God, has bestowed on you (Deut. 15:1-14).

In this passage there is no question of land to be left fallow, the stress is placed on "the remission of debts." If the Deuteronomist adopted for his own purposes the old legislation about the liberation of slaves during the seventh year, he largely expanded it and also included the remission of debts contracted by the poor, pledges, loans, etc.

But the Deuteronomist did not fail to add his favorite theme and to lift the obligation to the plane of religion:

> For remember that you too were once slaves in the land of Egypt, and the Lord, your God, ransomed you. That is why I am giving you this command today (Deut. 15:15).

Even after the social prescription that slaves be freed and debts be remitted became a religious prescription, it was connected with the liberation of the people from Egypt. The Jew freed his slave and forgave the poor their debts because he himself had once been poor and when he was a slave he had been freed.

But this law was not widely obeyed, largely because of the selfishness of the rich, and the Jewish economy failed to solve the problem of poverty. Therefore the punishment announced by Jeremias was not slow in coming. Because the people disobeyed the law about the land to be left fallow for a year, God Himself caused the land to be left fallow for many years:

> That every man should let his man-servant, and every man his maid-servant, being a Hebrew man or a Hebrew woman, go free: and that they should not lord it over them, to wit, over the Jews their brethren.
> And all the princes and all the people who entered into the covenant heard that every man should let his man-servant and every man his maid-servant go free and should no more have dominion over them. And they obeyed and let them

> go free. But afterwards they turned, and brought back again their servants and their handmaidens, whom they had let go free, and brought them into subjection as men-servants and maid-servants. And the word of the Lord came to Jeremias from the Lord, saying: Thus saith the Lord the God of Israel: I made a covenant with your fathers in the day that I brought them out of the land of Egypt, out of the house of bondage, saying:
>
> At the end of seven years, let ye go every man his brother, being a Hebrew, who hath been sold to thee, so he shall serve thee six years: and thou shalt let him go free from thee. And your fathers did not hearken to me, nor did they incline their ear.
>
> And you turned today and did that which was right in my eyes, in proclaiming liberty every one to his brother: and you made a covenant in my sight, in the house upon which my name is invocated. And you are fallen back and have defiled my name: and you have brought back again every man his man-servant, and every man his maid-servant, whom you had let go free and set at liberty: and you have brought them into subjection to be your servants and handmaids.
>
> Therefore thus saith the Lord: You have not hearkened to me in proclaiming liberty every man to his brother and every man to his friend: behold I proclaim a liberty for you, saith the Lord, to the sword, to the pestilence and to the famine: and I will cause you to be removed to all the kingdoms of the earth (Jer. 34:9-17).

Passages such as this and the many prophetic invectives suggest that the law about the liberation of slaves and the remission of debts was rarely obeyed and the sabbatical year was a total failure. When Leviticus, in a priestly document, legislated about the sabbatical year, care was taken to preserve these prescriptions and to return to the old law about fallow lands as laid down in the Covenant code. But a new kind of sabbatical year was created. This was the year of jubilee to which was assigned an enlarged version of the regulations specified by the Deuteronomist about the remission of debts. Let us limit ourselves to the paragraph about the land to be left fallow every sabbatical year:

> The Lord said to Moses on Mount Sinai, "Speak to the Israelites and tell them: when you enter the land that I am giving you, let the land, too, keep a sabbath for the Lord. For six years you may sow your field, and for six years prune your vineyard, gathering in their produce. But during the seventh year the land shall have a complete rest, a sabbath for the Lord, when you may neither sow your field nor prune your vineyard. The aftergrowth of your harvest you shall not reap, nor shall you pick the grapes of your untrimmed vines in this year of sabbath rest for the land. While the land has its sabbath, all its produce will be food equally for you yourself and for your male and female slaves, for your hired help and the tenants who live with you, and likewise for your livestock and for the wild animals on your land (Lev. 25:1-7).

This text suggests that a regression has taken place. Unlike the law in Deuteronomy, it repeats the old law about fallow land. A more careful reading, however, shows that this is more than an agrarian decree. Yet it would have been better to require the annual rotation of fallow land. If it was required that the land be left fallow for a whole year at a time, this was in order for the Jews to be sustained by "the sabbath of the land" itself. What does this mean? It means that during this year the Jews would once again live the life of a nomad, taking food wherever he could find it for himself and his flock. One year out of every seven he would cease to be a farmer who cultivated his own fields, and he would become a nomad. This is the religious secret of the sabbatical year, and it confirms something we have noted throughout our investigation. When agrarian rites were introduced into a nomadic setting, the Jewish rites and feasts were orientated toward the desert experience. It was during those years that the Jew had learned to be detached from himself and from the land he cultivated and which had made him rich. It was then that he renounced an easy and self-centered way of life in order that he might place himself in a covenant relationship with God who had chosen a people journeying towards promised happiness.

We may wonder how much of this was understood by the majority of the Hebrews. It can be granted that they celebrated the feast of Tents and that for eight days each year they lived like nomadic pilgrims and recalled the memory of their stay in the desert. It is harder to believe that they were willing to live like this for a whole year. Yet it matters little for our purpose to evaluate the measure of the popularity of such a regulation. It is sufficient to notice that the stages of the spiritualization of a feast are always the same. First the feast is an agrarian one, then it becomes nomadic. First it is on the plane of nature, then it is given an historical value.

B. THE JUBILEE YEAR

Although the priestly legislation no longer insisted on the liberation of slaves and the remission of debts every seven years, it did require that these prescriptions be most rigorously observed during the jubilee year which was celebrated every fifty years. Just as Pentecost, a week of seven weeks, was superimposed upon the weekly Sabbath, so the jubilee year, after seven weeks of years, was superimposed upon the sabbatical year. (It has been suggested that this jubilee year was not a full calendar year, but the lapse of time needed to reconcile the lunar year with the perpetual solar year.)

Let us first read the text of the new legislation. In it we may detect some traces of older texts recorded by the priests.

> Seven weeks of years shall you count—seven times seven years—so that the seven cycles amount to forty-nine years. Then on the tenth day of the seventh month let the trumpet resound; on this, the Day of Atonement, the trumpet blast shall re-echo throughout your land. This fiftieth year you shall make sacred by proclaiming liberty in the land for all its inhabitants. It shall be a jubilee for you when every one of you shall return to his own property, every one to his own family estate. In this fiftieth year, your year of jubilee, you shall not sow, nor shall you reap the aftergrowth or pick the grapes from the untrimmed vines. Since this is the jubilee, which shall be sacred for you, you may not eat of its produce, except as taken directly from the field.
>
> In this year of jubilee, then, every one of you shall return to his own property. Therefore, when you sell any land to your neighbor or buy any from him, do not deal unfairly. On the basis of the number of years since the last jubilee shall you purchase the land from him; and so also, on the basis of the number of years for crops, shall he sell it to you (Lev. 25:8-16).

The object of this prescription is to restore to their original owners during the fiftieth year, all lands purchased during the preceding forty-nine years. Actually this meant that all exchange of land was by way of rent and not purchase. In this way, it was hoped that landowners would never lose their patrimony and would retain the family heritage forever. The priestly legislation attached great importance to this point. Yet in the economic and social context some religious values were introduced. These were significant for the future evolution of the jubilee year. First of all, there was the concept that the land belonged to God. This was the ultimate reason why it could not be definitely alienated. Then, there was the concept of "redemption" that is implied in the regulation about the jubilee year. This meant that a family possession had to be "redeemed," preferably by a kinsman (the *goel*) lest it fall into the hands of someone outside the family. Lastly, there was the concept of the remission not only of the remission of debts, but also of sins. This was faintly suggested by the fact that the jubilee year opened on the tenth day of the seventh month, the day of expiation. In this way a connection was established between the remission of debts and the remission of sins.

These three ideas are most important, even though they are only suggested in the text of Leviticus. The prophets made them the basis of their teaching, safeguarding and prolonging the life of the institution in this way and giving to it an eschatological orientation in which these ideas would become even more spiritual.

This eschatological orientation should be attributed to Isaias. He described the messianic age, the era of the last days, as a jubilee year:

> The spirit of the Lord is upon me, because the Lord hath anointed me. He hath sent me to preach to the meek, to heal the contrite of heart, and to preach a release to the captives and deliverance to them that are shut up:
>
> To proclaim the acceptable year of the Lord and the day of vengeance of our God: to comfort all that mourn:
>
> To appoint to the mourners of Sion: and to give them a crown for ashes, the oil of joy for mourning, a garment of praise for the spirit of grief. And they shall be called in it the mighty ones of justice, the planting of the Lord to glorify him (Is. 61:1-3).

The opening of this jubilee year is announced not with the blast of a trumpet but with the words of the prophet. The announcement is significantly called the "good news," an expression which in our Christian language has become the "gospel," as if the essence of the gospel is the proclamation of the Lord's year of grace. The content of this year of grace resembles the content of the jubilee years: amnesty for prisoners, freedom for slaves, credit for debtors. Furthermore, the remission of debts also became the remission of sins, and in the messianic age the Lord is represented as the *goel* who would redeem men from their sins:

> And there shall come a redeemer to Sion and to them that return from iniquity in Jacob, saith the Lord (Is. 59:20). Neither shall he that is near say: I am feeble. The people that dwell therein shall have their iniquity taken away from them (Is. 33:24).

The first discourse with which the Lord inaugurated His public life was a commentary on the Isaian text proclaiming a spiritual jubilee year. Christ paraphrased it in these words:

> The Spirit of the Lord is upon me because he has anointed me, to bring good news to the poor he has sent me, to proclaim to the captives release, and sight to the blind; to set at liberty the oppressed, to proclaim the acceptable year of the Lord, and the day of recompense. . . . Today this Scripture has been fulfilled in your hearing (Lk. 18-19, 21).

Therefore we can conclude that Christ looked on His ministry as a true jubilee year. He proved this many times when He cited texts from the prophecy of Isaias to justify His actions (Mt. 11:2-6; Lk. 1:77; 4:21). He made His meaning very clear when He exercised His power of forgiving sins, to the scandal of the Pharisees:

> And behold some of the Scribes said within themselves, "This man blasphemes." And Jesus, knowing their thoughts, said, "Why do you harbor evil thoughts in your hearts? For which is easier, to say, 'Thy sins are forgiven thee' or to say, 'Arise and walk'? But that you may know that the Son of Man has power on earth to forgive sins"—then he said to the paralytic—"Arise, take up thy pallet and go to thy house" (Mt. 9:3-6).

Christ's public ministry consisted of an uninterrupted series of liberations, cures, remission of debts and of sins. When He returned to the Father, He took care to place this jubilee power to forgive sins in the Sunday liturgy, entrusting it to the Apostles when He first appeared to them and gave them the Spirit, that is, the messianic Spirit:

> When he had said this, he breathed upon them and said to them, "Receive the Holy Spirit; whose sins you shall forgive, they are forgiven them; and whose sins you shall retain, they are retained" (Jn. 20:22-23).

In fact, this spiritual jubilee year, whose graces are contained in our Sunday, opened with a day of expiation just like the old levitical jubilee year:

> All of you drink of this; for this is my blood of the new covenant, which is being shed for many unto the forgiveness of sins (Mt. 26:27-28).

We need look no further than the celebration of Sunday to find evidences of the sabbatical and the jubilee year in Christianity. On that day, debts are forgiven, freedom is enjoyed, and the blessings of the messianic era became present realities.

Chapter Ten

Votive Feasts

We have completed our examination of the feasts and celebrations connected with the Sabbath; we shall now consider a final group of votive feasts. These were admitted to the calendar very late and never became popular. Our discussion can be brief because only one had any influence on the theology of New Testament feasts.

A. THE DEDICATION OF THE TEMPLE

The first feast to be considered is that of the dedication of the temple. This feast commemorates not Solomon's great consecration of the temple (3 Kgs. 8), but the consecration made by the Machabees.

It was customary to commemorate the consecration of Solomon's temple on the feast of Tents and it is not unlikely that the superimposition of this new object upon an old agrarian feast contributed to its spiritualization. In fact, it seems that the commemoration of the dwelling of the people in tents during the years spent in the desert also recalled Yahweh's stay amidst His people under the "tent"—the tabernacle. There is even a tradition that Yahweh manifested a certain disdain for the temple and expressed a preference for the tent. There was always the danger that the people, because of the temple, would settle down and forget the nomadic conditions of their existence (1 Kgs. 7:5-7).

David was not allowed to build a temple for God because the moment had not yet come. The temple suggested a permanent dwelling, but the people were meant to recall that they must always be ready to break camp, and at all times they must be prepared to carry out their God's commands.

Solomon probably thought the whole question was settled when he built the temple and consecrated it with a prodigious number of sacrifices. But it is significant that the Tent of Reunion was carried into the temple during the rite of consecration.

> Then all the ancients of Israel with the princes of the tribes, and the heads of the families of the children of Israel were assembled to king Solomon in Jerusalem: that they might carry the ark of the covenant of the Lord out of the city of David, that is, out of Sion.
>
> And all Israel assembled themselves to king Solomon on the festival day in the month of Ethanim: the same is the seventh month.

> And all the ancients of Israel came: and the priests took up the ark, and carried the ark of the Lord, and the tabernacle of the covenant, and all the vessels of the sanctuary, that were in the tabernacle. And the priests and the Levites carried them . . . . And the priests brought in the ark of the covenant of the Lord into its place, into the oracle of the temple into the Holy of Holies under the wings of the cherubims (3 Kgs. 8:1-4, 6).

Consequently, at the heart of the solid, well-built temple, God took care still to dwell in a tent and to accompany the ark, the traditional chest of the nomad. The narrator points out that the temple was consecrated in the feast of the seventh month, that is on the feast of Tabernacles with all its associations with the years spent in the desert.

When the schismatic king of the northern tribes wished to duplicate the temple of Solomon so that his people would not go up to Jerusalem, he used the ritual of the feast of Tabernacles for the consecration ceremony:

> And he appointed a feast in the eighth month, on the fifteenth day of the month, after the manner of the feast that was celebrated in Juda. And going up to the altar, he did in like manner in Bethel, to sacrifice to the calves, which he had made. And he placed in Bethel priests of the high places, which he had made (3 Kgs. 12:32).

To the different themes of the feast of Tabernacles, of Tents, which we have studied in an earlier chapter, we should now add the theme of the dwelling of the Lord in the tent in the midst of His people. The tent and the ark seem to have disappeared at the time of the Exile. The prophets noted this and declared that the future messiah would one day make His dwelling in a magnificent tent that would be brought to this earth. In this connection we can, perhaps, understand Peter's desire to erect a tent for the transfigured Christ in whom he recognized the expected messiah (Mt. 17:4).

Long after the Exile, in Machabean days, the feast of the Dedication was instituted. This was a separate feast, and it had no connection with the feast of Tents. The new feast commemorated the restoration of the temple after its profanation. Yet if we compare the various Scripture passages with certain descriptions of the ritual, we will find that the ceremony chosen was that of the feast of Tents. Even if the feast of the Dedication was celebrated in the tenth month, sight was not lost in the fixed and stable building of the nomadic tent (1 Mach. 4:1-59).

> Then Judas and his brethren said: Behold our enemies are discomfited: let us go up now to cleanse the holy places and to repair them. And all the army assembled together and they went up into Mount Sinai. . . . And he chose priests without blemish whose will was set upon the law of God. And they cleansed the holy places and took away the stones that had been defiled into an unclean place. . . . And they put incense upon the altar and lighted the lamps that were upon the candlestick and they gave light in the temple. . . . And Judas and his brethren and all the church of Israel decreed, that the day of the dedication of the altar should be kept in its season from year to year, for eight days, from the five and twentieth day of the month of Casleu, with joy and gladness (1 Mach. 4:36-37, 42, 43, 50, 59).

Here we find in this ritual the chief elements of the feast of Tents: the rite of expiation (more important at this moment than ever before because of the profanation), joy, crowns, light. Other texts suggest further details, for example the water libations:

> And when the sacrifice was consumed, Nehemias commanded the water that was left to be poured out upon the great stones (2 Mach. 1:31).

The ritual was taken from the feast of Tents:

> And they kept eight days with joy, after the manner of the feast of the tabernacles, remembering that not long before they had kept the feast of the tabernacles when they were in the mountains and in dens, like wild beasts. Therefore they now carried boughs and green branches and palms for Him that had given them good success in cleansing his place. And they ordained by a common statute and decree that all the nation of the Jews should keep those days every year (2 Mach. 10:6-8).

Even in the month of December green boughs and palms were used to establish the connection between the feast of the Dedication and the feast of Tents and to denote the same mystery of God's dwelling in the midst of a people who were on their way to heaven.

Christ once went up to Jerusalem on the feast of Dedication, and during an argument with the Pharisees, He declared that He was "the consecrated" of the Father (Jn. 10:36). But we can best understand Christ's thought about the temple if we study His words and actions when He drove out those who were buying and selling in its courts. Obviously the Lord wished to "personalize" the feast in His own bodv.

> "Destroy this temple and in three days I will raise it up" (Jn. 2:19).

The dedication of the altar is meaningless unless a spiritual sacrifice is offered there. A spiritual sacrifice is the attitude of a soul charged with sacrificial values. The temple is now to be found in the Christ. It is also to be found in each Christian who celebrates the true feast of the Dedication by offering himself to God as the temple of the Holy Spirit:

> I exhort you therefore, brethren, by the mercy of God, to present your bodies as a sacrifice, living, holy, pleasing to God—your spiritual service (Rom. 12:1).

B. THE FEAST OF LOTS

We shall refer briefly to this feast which was always profane in character and had no connection with the New Testament. In early days it was probably connected with the feast of the New Year and must have been separated from it sometime during the Persian period. The book of Esther describes a ceremony of drawing lots such as was often practiced by pagans at the beginning of the year. We alluded to this when we described the new-year ritual in an earlier chapter.

> In the first month (which is called Nisan) in the twelfth year of the reign of Assuerus, the lot was cast into an urn, which in Hebrew is called Phur, before Aman, on what day and what month the nation of the Jews should be destroyed. And there came out the twelfth month, which is caller Adar (Esth. 3:7).

On this occasion the lots revealed that the Jews would be massacred on the third day of the twelfth month.

Thanks to Esther's efforts, the Jews were spared and their enemies were punished. Thereafter the feast of Lots was observed as a Jewish feast by the Jews who lived in Persia. Paralleling the pagan feasts, there were excessively convivial banquets, the exchange of gifts and the book of Esther was read in the synagogue.

However, the Palestinian Jews long hesitated to adopt this feast because of its profane nature and they never made any effort to celebrate it in the temple.

C. FAST DAYS

Fasting is an old Jewish custom. But it was always a private matter, whether it was inspired by private devotion or was part of a communal celebration. It became important in times of trouble and disappeared when all was going well. David, it will be remembered, fasted when his child was ill:

> And he said: While the child was yet alive, I fasted and wept for him. For I said: Who knoweth whether the Lord may not give him to me, and the child may live? But now that he is dead, why should I fast? Shall I be able to bring him back any more? I shall go to him rather: but he shall not return to me (2 Kgs. 12:22-23).

In early days fasting was always associated with a specific misfortune: for example, after a defeat (Judg. 20:26), after a death (1 Kgs. 31:13; 2 Kgs. 1:12; 3:35), as a proof of conversion (2 Kgs. 12:16; 3 Kgs. 21:27). But these efforts were personal rather than liturgical, even when the fast lasted seven days (Gen. 50:10; 1 Kgs. 31:13).

There were many examples of collective fasting at the time of the disasters connected with the Exile. When they were in distant lands, the people substituted commemorative fasts for their traditional feasts. From this time, fasting could be said to be part of the liturgy, in fact it regularly commemorated some past misfortune just as a rite commemorated events connected with salvation.

A fast was arranged for the beginning of the tenth month to commemorate the beginning of the siege of Jerusalem (4 Kgs. 25:1; cf. Zach. 8:19). Another fast recalled the breach made in the rampart in the fourth month (4 Kgs. 25:4; Zach. 8:19). The capture of Jerusalem in the fifth month was also transformed into a day of fast (4 Kgs. 25:8; Zach. 7:3). The same thing was done for the day on which Godolias was assassinated in the seventh month (4 Kgs. 25:25; Zach. 7:5; 8:19). Thus fasting became a rite in which the Jew placed himself in a state of personal distress in order to present himself to God in this state and to ask to be delivered.

The possible formalism of such an attitude can be imagined. In Isaias we are warned of the struggle against this tendency and reminded that fasting should be accompanied by charity if it is to be truly pleasing to God:

> Why have we fasted: and thou hast not regarded? Have we humbled our souls: and thou hast not taken notice? Behold in the day of your fast your own will is found: and you exact of all your debtors. Behold you fast for debates and

> strife, and strike with fist wickedly. Do not fast as you have done until this day, to make your cry to be heard on high. Is this such a fast as I have chosen: For a man to afflict his soul for a day? Is this it: To wind his head about like a circle and to spread sackcloth and ashes? Wilt thou call this a fast and a day acceptable to the Lord? Is not this rather the fast that I have chosen? Loosen the bands of wickedness, undo the bundles that oppress. Let them that are broken go free: and break asunder every burden. Deal thy bread to the hungry and bring the needy and the harbourless into thy house: when thou shalt see one naked, cover him and despise not thy own flesh (Is. 58:3-7).

When the Exile came to an end, the people came to consult Zacharias to ask if they should continue to observe the fasts that had been introduced during their years of misfortune:

> And it came to pass in the fourth year of king Darius, that the word of the Lord came to Zacharias, in the fourth day of the ninth month, which is Casleu. When Sarasar and Rogommelech and the men that were with him sent to the house of God, to entreat the face of the Lord: To speak to the priests of the house of the Lord of hosts and to the prophets saying: Must I weep in the fifth month or must I sanctify myself as I have now done for many years? And the word of the Lord of hosts came to me, saying: Speak to all the people of the land and to the priests, saying: When you fasted and mourned in the fifth and the seventh month for these seventy years, did you keep a fast unto me? . . . Thus saith the Lord of hosts, saying: Judge ye true judgement and shew ye mercy and compassion every man to his brother. And oppress not the widow and the fatherless and the stranger and the poor . . . (Zach. 7:1-8).

The prophet insisted on the unimportance of fasting. Whether a man fasted or not meant little in the sight of God, who looks for charity and justice. Fasting disappeared. Days of fast became days of joy and gladness. Charity always remained obligatory:

> Thus saith the Lord of hosts: The fast of the fourth month and the fast of the fifth and the fast of the seventh and the fast of the tenth shall be to the house of Juda joy and gladness and great solemnities: only love ye truth and peace (Zach. 8:19).

The first postexilic prophets resisted the practice of fasting for its own sake. Some asked whether it were necessary to fast, now that everything was getting better. Others wondered why they should become involved in complicated fasting rites, if God preferred charity to fasting. Fortunately, at this stage of its development, fasting, although it became enmeshed in extravagent formalism, followed the same evolution as that of feasts and rites. It began to commemorate historical events, especially disasters of the past. But it also expressed an attitude of the soul of the Jew, impoverished and humbled, who awaited the help of His Lord. It pointed to eschatological salvation. It prepared the way for God's action. Here we recognize the characteristic development of the principal liturgical feasts.

At a date difficult to determine, it was decided to suppress fasts commemorating incidents of the siege of Jerusalem and to replace them with the feast of Expiation (Yom Kippur) which became the most important fast of all. We discussed this fast when we spoke of the feast of Expiation in the ritual of the feast of Tents and of the New Year. In the priestly code we find this new aspect of a day of penance and fast:

> This shall be an everlasting ordinance for you: on the tenth day of the seventh month every one of you, whether a native or a resident alien, shall mortify himself and shall do no work. Since on this day atonement is made for you to make you clean, so that you may be cleansed of all your sins before the Lord, by everlasting ordinance it shall be a most solemn sabbath for you, on which you must mortify yourselves (Lev. 16:29-31; cf. 23:27-32; Num. 29:7-11).

There is no reason to disdain this feast. It expresses a sense of sin and shows an awareness of the need of help which God alone can give.

Fasting then increased to an extraordinary degree in the Jewish world. It became the principal characteristic of Judaism. To see this, it is necessary merely to read the principal texts of this period (Esth. 4:1-3, 16; 9:31; 14:2; Tob. 3:10-11; 12:8; Jud. 4:8-10; 8:6; 9:1; 12:9). The reason for this popularity is obvious. Fasting is the rite that best expresses the attitude of soul that is related to the sacrificial practices of the temple. The rabbis liked to say that fasting is the equivalent of placing on the altar the holocaust of one's own body and blood.[56] This statement helps us to understand the theology of the fast as a spiritual rite. Two texts in Joel throw light on this new interpretation. All the people are invited to an official fast which might well be part of a feast of Expiation. The description of the fast is detailed but there is no mention of any sacrificial immolation.

> Gird yourselves and lament, O ye priests: howl, ye ministers of the altars. Go in, lie in sackcloth, ye ministers of my God: because sacrifice and libation is cut off from the house

[56] *Bekaroth* II, pp. 6-8.

> of your God. Sanctify ye a fast, call an assembly, gather together the ancients, all the inhabitants of the land into the house of your God: and cry to the Lord (Joel 1:13-14). Now therefore saith the Lord: Be converted to me with all your heart, in fasting and in weeping and in mourning. And rend your hearts and not your garments, and turn to the Lord your God: for he is gracious and merciful, patient and rich in mercy, and ready to repent of the evil. Who knoweth but he will return and forgive and leave a blessing behind him, sacrifice and libation to the Lord your God? Blow the trumpet in Sion: sanctify the church, assemble the ancients, gather together the little ones and them that suck at the breasts: let the bridegroom go forth from his bed and the bride out of her bride chamber. Between the porch and the altar the priests the Lord's ministers shall weep and shall say: Spare, O Lord, spare thy people: and give not thy inheritance to reproach, that the heathen should rule over them. Why should they say among the nations: Where is their God? (Joel 2:12-17).

Unfortunately there were no more prophets who could repeatedly remind the people that in addition to the fast, it was the attitude of soul that was important. Later it would be hard to imagine the proclamation of a votive fast such as Joel had recommended. Everything was regimented. There was the feast of Yom Kippur and the two days of fast each week which the Pharisees had established—Monday and Thursday. The prophets' last attempts to spiritualize fasting had failed and formalism succeeded in putting an end to what they had accomplished.

When we examine the story of the life of our Lord, we see the chief elements of this Old Testament evolution in His attitude toward fasting. Christ began His work by fasting forty days (Mt. 4:1-11). Clearly this fast was meant to be related to the desert experience of the Israelites which it recapitulated. It was a memorial rite. Yet the importance of the fast is to be found not so much in the commemoration of an event that was far from perfect, but in the substitution of a new and altogether perfect event for the old one. Christ was the first to triumph over the desert temptations. His attitude of soul expressed itself perfectly in the rite and transcended it. In this spirit, the Lord repeated the teaching of the old prophets and rejected the formalistic fast:

> And when you fast, do not look gloomy like the hypocrites, who disfigure their faces in order to appear to men as fasting. Amen I say to you, they have received their reward. But thou, when thou dost fast, anoint thy head and wash thy face, so that thou mayest not be seen fasting by men, but by thy Father, who is in secret; and thy Father who sees in secret, will reward thee (Mt. 6:16-18).

This led to the proclamation of the relative character of penitential practices but not to their abrogation (Phil. 4:12-13; Eph. 5:28-29; 1 Cor. 6:15-19; Gal. 5:13). To stress the difference between Christian and Jewish fasting, the early Church chose new fast days:

> Let your fasts not take place at the same time as those used by the hypocrites (Didache 8:1).

The Christian fast became a rite that enabled each man to duplicate in his own soul Christ's attitude of soul when He was dying on the cross. His was a spiritual sacrifice completely one with the salvific action of the Father.

Conclusion

SUMMARY OF THE EVIDENCE

Summary

the Evolution of Feasts in the Bible

A. THE VALUE OF THE WORLD OF NATURE

Even though there are many breaks in continuity between Jewish and Christian liturgical feasts and rites, it should be admitted that Jewish worship was an important formative factor in the development of our Christian feasts.

If we go back still further we will find discrepancies between the feasts of the pagan and the Jewish world. Yet these differences are not intrinsic and do not negate the important bonds that unite the two worlds.

We should frankly face the inescapable fact that the revelation of God's plan does not include the creation of completely new feasts or the establishment of a completely new ritual which is in some way divinely inspired and brought from heaven to earth. There is, rather, a continuity between the human rite, which was the point of departure, and the Christian rite, which we now celebrate. This means a fidelity to the grace of the natural fact—a first and precious truth that we will do well to recall in our present catechesis of Christian feasts: we should move from the natural level to the supernatural.

To this basic fact of continuity, a series of correctives must be added which in no way jeopardize the fundamental principle of continuity. Easter is a feast of extraordinary power in the Church, but it is always celebrated in the spring and it remains, on its own sublime height, a feast of renewal. Sunday follows the weekly rhythm established both by Eastern astrologers and the recurrence of the Jewish Sabbath; and, although the words do not denote the same reality, it is a day of rest and a day of freedom, a day which is lifted above the work-day level of the other six days of the week.

The community assembly, a pilgrim people on the march, water, light, fruit, unleavened bread, enthronement rites—all these were more and more purified, more and more spiritualized so that they might serve as the common denominator for pagan, Jewish, and Christian feasts.

B. LIMITATIONS OF THE FEASTS OF NATURE

All man-made and pagan feasts did not become part of the worship of the people of God. Far from it. Some of them were incorporated in the Jewish liturgy and then disappeared, unable to undergo the necessary spiritualization. It is hard to imagine a Jew observing the idolatrous feasts of the Sumerian world. Nor can we conceive of a Christian, freed from the servitude of the elements of the world, honoring the new moon. We can even go so far as to say that no pagan or Jewish feast was ever moved unchanged into the Christian calendar. It would, however, be more correct to say that these feasts entered this calendar only after dying with Christ and being reborn to a new existence in the Christian Sunday. At any rate, it cannot be denied that the Jewish feasts which were incorporated into Christian liturgy were at first connected with Sunday. The Sabbath was associated with Christ's death because the rest it prescribed recalled Christ's rest in the tomb so that He might be reborn on Sunday. Even Easter and Pentecost came into Christianity only in connection with the Sunday on which they were celebrated. The year of Jubilee and its time of grace was the first festival that was not related to the Sunday.

In other words, for a Jewish or pagan feast to exist as a Christian feast, it was necessary that it be able to express in some way Christ's death and resurrection. That this was true of Easter and Sunday is evident. It also applies to the theme of water which was originally connected with the feast of Tents and which John observed flowing from the side of Christ crucified. As a matter of fact, it is impossible for a ceremony with a natural signification to enter our liturgy unless it announces Christ's death and unless it itself experienced this "dying" and this "rebirth" in the history of its own spiritualization. The Sabbath is dead; yet transfigured it can be recognized in the Sunday. The traditional Jewish feast is dead and Christ sealed this death by adopting a a special ritual and chronology; yet it remains mysteriously present in our Christian celebration of the unleavened bread and the lamb.

C. AGARIAN AND NOMADIC RITES

Throughout our investigation we have observed a latent conflict between two kinds of different rites, in fact, between two different cultures: the agrarian world into which Israel came and the nomadic world from which it emerged. The huts of the feast of the Harvest became nomadic tents, the unleavened bread of the first days of the harvest became the bread of those who travel in haste, the fallow fields of the seventh year marked a return to a nomad's attitude toward land. So we find a principle of selection operating even here in the concurrence between rites of different origin. Only those rites were gradually purified and reached the term of their evolution in Christianity which were originally nomadic rites and feasts (for example, the paschal lamb), or were agrarian rites and feasts which could be "reread" as a function of a nomadic situation (for example, the sojourn in the desert). This suggests that although all our Christian rites are derived from natural rites, it is not correct to conclude that every natural rite can be introduced into our liturgy: agrarian rites, bourgeois or urban customs have never had a long liturgical life. Therefore, we may formulate the first law for the spiritualization of natural rites: they must belong to a nomadic culture or at least be able to be integrated in terms of a nomadic culture. We shall soon see the reason for this requirement. For the moment, let us observe that it follows that many agrarian rites, such as the offering of sheaves, thanksgiving for harvests and reaping, presentation of first fruits, cease to have a liturgical role.

D. THE EVENT OF THE STAY IN THE DESERT

The old pagan feasts, agrarian or astronomical, were fundamentally an effort to express man's desire to enter into the regular rhythm of the world and the stars. A well-observed new moon celebration put man in harmony with the coming month. A well-observed new year celebration which included the casting of lots and the enthronement of the year's god-king, ensured happiness, provided man could conform his will to the will of the god. Jewish rites and feasts are original in that they combine this natural rhythm of the world with another rhythm. Jewish feasts relate the faithful with the event of the stay in the desert, from the liberation of the people from Egypt until the entrance into the promised land. This includes the promulgation of the law, the incident of the rock of living water and the dwelling of the Lord in the midst of His people. This new concept of a feast is important from more than one point of view and denotes an interesting advance in the spiritualization of Jewish rites. When man took part in a Jewish feast, he placed himself not only in harmony with nature but in harmony with history itself. The history, as a matter of fact, knows nothing of the fatalism of nature in which all is gratuitous. Moreover, in raising himself to the level of history, the Jew makes room for the initiative of God and His control of this history. The rite ceases to be cyclical, in the manner of natural rites; it is now charged with freedom and gift.

All this advance helped the Jewish people to transcend the natural rites and to "reread" them so as to see how they signified the historic event of the stay in the desert. It is startling to see how these rites with their very plain natural significance came to denote the event of salvation. The unleavened bread used in agrarian rites recalled the haste of the departure from Egypt. The sets of seven in the perpetual calendar gave dignity to the feast of Weeks which became the memorial of the promulgation of the Law. Lest the stability and solidity of the temple building engross men's attention, God came to dwell above the tabernacle at the time of its consecration, just as He had during the years of wandering in the desert. The libations with their accompanying wonders at the annual celebration of the feast of Tents recalled the rock of living water. In like manner, the custom of fallow fields was another reminder of nomadic days when the people were dependent on whatever growing things they found along their way. The Sabbath recalled the weekly "cessation" of manna. The harvests signified the fertility of the land God gave His people. The custom of "the remission of debts" was a recognition of God's exclusive rights over the earth. Lastly, the Sabbath-day liberty enjoyed by slaves was a sign of the liberation from Egypt.

It follows that a whole series of feasts will be suppressed: all those that belong to an astronomical cycle (especially new-moon feasts) that cannot be related to an event.

The extent of the spiritualization of natural rites systematically applied by the Jewish people in the Deuteronomic reform is startling. These natural rites continued in a transformed state to which the "rereading" gave a new consistency because it lifted them from a natural level to the historical level. Whenever the people met in a liturgical assembly, they recalled their Covenant assemblies in the desert, and whenever they experienced the need of renewing the Covenant and of achieving closer union with Yahweh, this was expressed within the framework of the old agrarian feasts which now became a memorial of the desert to be sealed in the renewal of the Covenant.

E. LITURGICAL CATECHESIS

Obviously this spiritualization was not a sudden thing. On the contrary, it was the result of years of meditation and of prophetic activity. All this was concretized in the Deuteronomic reform accelerated by the prophets of the eighth century and their disciples. It was God's Word that forced the people to make this rereading and it is this same Word that maintained the rite in its new meaning. As long as the meaning of the rite was natural and obvious, no words were needed. The rite explained itself and effected what it signified. But as soon as the spiritualization of the feast began and it was lifted to a plane higher than the natural plane or the one on which it was celebrated, it was necessary that it be accompanied by the Word so that the new meaning be maintained and the relation to the historic event be specifically stated. As soon as a rite evolves, no matter how faithfully it preserves natural values, it should be explained. We have noted the introduction of the first liturgical catechesis in the family Passover ceremony, on the day when the lamb and the unleavened bread acquired a new meaning.

There is no reason for us to be surprised in our twentieth century because some of our Christian rites no longer speak to our people. This is a normal law and is the result of their spiritualization. But a catechesis and the constant reference of the rite to the event and to the Word is the normal law of a liturgy based on spiritualized rites. The commentary on these rites becomes an essential part of the liturgy the moment that they move from the natural plane to the plane of faith.

F. THE MYSTERY

It was not enough for a reference to be made during a feast to the incidents that took place in the desert to ensure that a rite would survive with its new symbolism. Time and again, the prophets complained that the people showed little interest in their past history and were powerfully drawn to the worship of Baal. Therefore, it was necessary to arouse the interest of the Jew in an event that had occurred many centuries earlier. It was the Deuteronomist theology that orchestrated, if it did not invent, the idea of the reactualization of the past event in the rite. This does not mean that we should examine this theology through the eyes of a Christian, much less through those of a Casel. Yet, it is nonetheless true that in celebrating the feast of the Passover, the Jew no longer restricted himself to the memory of the long distant passage from Egypt to the Promised Land. He believed that at that very moment the Lord stretched out His arms to save him.

Obviously this spiritualization meant the elimination of a number of rites which could not be given the new dimension. For example, the immolation of the paschal lamb, in its original form, with all its vague allusions to the ancient magic nomadic rite could not be purified without significant changes. So it was transformed in Deuteronomist theology into the family paschal meal which was introduced at this time. It was indeed this family, as the father reminded his child, that had been brought out of Egypt. . .

Most rites and feasts were modified along these lines at this time. When the Jew moved into a tent for eight days, he no longer wished to repeat an ancient historical act but to introduce once again into his own life the values of expendability and detachment inherent in the nomadic experience. This was even more true when the Jew found himself, one year out of seven, dependent like a nomad on the products of the soil. This desire to "re-actualize" feasts explains how Jewish feasts became the occasion for periodic renewals of the Covenant. In this way the feast not only commemorated the Covenant, but repeated it, renewed it and brought its blessings to those who took part and enabled them to benefit from the soteriological power of the ancient events.

The most typical case of reactualization is undoubtedly to be found in the days of fast introduced during the Exile and whose aim was to recall the stages of the seige of Jerusalem. Each time the Jew fasted, he truly took upon himself in some way the disastrous events of the past. He identified himself with them and presented himself before his God to win pardon and freedom. Is it not in a context like this that the theology of the suffering servant who took upon himself the deeds and faults of his people could have been fashioned?

G. ATTITUDE OF HEART

When the rite had been purified to the point that it actualized the historical event and enabled the individual who celebrated it to share in the unfolding of God's plan in history, then the individual or the people observing the feast were required to reproduce an attitude of heart similar to or perhaps more perfect than that of their ancestors. Another advance could be noted when the people introduced into their theology of time the past infidelities of their people. To observe a feast properly, it became necessary to meet additional demands.

Very early the Israelites had been taught to look upon the Sabbath as a day on which justice should be shown to slaves, and they had always regarded this as the "sign" of the Covenant. This was indeed a curious transposition of the pagan rest-taboo into a rest with social and moral dimensions. In this perspective the day of expiation acquired a new significance and the jubilee year tended to become a year for the remission of sin. Eager to preserve the practice of fasting from all taint of formalism, the prophets made it the basic element of the new liturgical year and they insisted that when soul and heart are also involved, fasting becomes far more efficacious than sacrifices which entail the shedding of blood. It was understood that a year should not pass without the observance of several days of fast.

In this way the Jewish feast aroused the appropriate interior attitude and made the response part of the rite itself. It was the people's present attitude of heart that became the object of the celebration. The history of the ancient salvific events was prolonged in personal attitudes.

Unhappily, Judaism did not possess the dynamism required to realize in all its plenitude this new stage of spiritualization. The meticulous human prescriptions of the Pharisees succeeded, finally, in strangling the spirit for the sake of the letter. On the borders of Judaism this movement was to be carried still further. In the Qumran community, in the perpetual calendar of Jubilees, etc., the liturgical year developed outside the official setting. No use of the traditional rites of the paschal lamb and the unleavened bread or of the temple was made. All the emphasis was placed on the attitude of heart of the participants.

Christ, in favor of the perpetual calendar, celebrated the Passover with little reference to the rite but with careful insistence on the proper attitude of soul. He achieved the object of the feast in a uniquely perfect way through His obedience to the Father, His acceptance of death, His desire to save all men, His hope of new life. His attitude was so perfect that no other rites were needed; Christ Himself is the lamb, He Himself is the head, He Himself is "our pasch." Thus the feast became personified in the Person of Christ Himself. The feast became a person.

Christ's spiritual defense of the Sabbath against the Pharisees revealed both the "God who works" and the "Master of the Sabbath." His many journeys to Jerusalem and His presence at the principal Jewish feasts usually culminated in a warning addressed to those taking part in the feasts and alerted them to the danger of false ritualism which was now stripped of all meaning. At the same time, He revealed that He is the new rite because He observed the feast of the Passover in His paschal attitude; He is the rock of living water of the feast of Tents; He is the temple, spotlessly pure and needing no purification;

He is the King who is enthroned during the new-year feast.

Yet merely to say that, in Christ's Person, all Jewish rites were fulfilled would be to minimize His role. It is not enough to say that Christ is the true messiah awaited in the feasts of the new moon. Christ is not only the object of the feasts, He is the feast itself, in the measure in which the feast, going beyond the rite, became an attitude of soul. We run the risk of seeing nothing more in the Johannine images, say, than beautiful symbols, while actually they contain a deep reality and orchestrate an authentic christology. It was Christ's intention, in celebrating the Jewish feasts, not merely to declare that He was the object of the feast, but rather to give these feasts their maximum tension and to lift them to the level of His own paschal drama.

Lastly, before it was possible for these feasts to attain a still greater spiritualization, it was necessary for them to express not merely an attitude of soul but the inner attitude of Christ Himself in His paschal drama. This includes His passage from death to life, His obedience to the Father, His suffering for the salvation of the world, His lordship over life and death. Certain feasts disappeared precisely because they were unable to signify this paschal drama. The feast of Tents was eliminated from the liturgical year because the life it celebrated was not sufficiently a life born of death; the harvest it extolled was not sufficiently the fruit of the seed dying in the earth.

On the other hand, fasting was discovered to be particularly appropriate as an efficacious memorial of the death of the Lord. Just as this fasting was a memorial of the misfortunes that befell Jerusalem under the old Covenant, so it found a place in the two days of the week associated with two stages of Christ's death: the day on which He was delivered up to be crucified (Wednesday) and the day on which He died (Friday). The Jewish Passover feast continued in a new setting. Just as Christ celebrated the Passover on the margin of the official calendar so as to free it the more easily from the old ritual constraints, so the Church placed the whole Passover feast on a Sunday, in order to prolong Christ's act and to teach us to see that the attitude of soul is more important than the rite itself.

H. THE ASSEMBLY FOR THE FEAST

From time immemorial the Jewish feast had been celebrated at the close of a pilgrimage which brought the whole people to the mountain of Jerusalem. Thus the feast provided an opportunity for a renewal of awareness of the communal values of the holy people. This does not merely mean that individuals with the same attitude prayed side by side, but rather that when they celebrated the feast together they began to acquire a new awareness of their national conscience. When they refrained from servile work on the Sabbath, they realized once again that they were a free people whom God had delivered from

Egyptian slavery. When they went up to Jerusalem for the three great feasts of the year, they expressed their acceptance of God's plan for the world, and they ratified their acceptance by renewing the Covenant which united them more closely than ever before with God's life. So the Sabbath was understood to be the "sign" of this shared life; on this day the people rested just as God did, and expressed this privilege by putting aside every worldly kind of life, by taking part in divine worship, and by meditating on His law. There was a still more important consequence that must be noted. When the tribes assembled in Jerusalem on a feast day (as a rule this meant that only a few tribes were able to come together at one time), they were reminded that it was their mission to assemble all the nations and lead them to the holy city to celebrate the same feast and acclaim the sovereignty of the God of Israel.

But there was still too much of this world about the assembly for it to be called a truly divine convocation. It consisted of too many human practices for it to be an authentic *ecclesia*. That is why Christ convoked another kind of assembly, one that meets every Sunday so that its members can await His coming and exercise the messianic powers with which He endowed it. Here, for the first time in the history of the world, men of every race and tongue, through the rite of expiation realized by the Lord, can be purified from their sins and through His resurrection enter into the life of the Son of God.

I. GOD FIRST

A pagan feast is essentially an act of homage made by man to his god, a gesture of gratitude or adoration or supplication which rises from earth to heaven. It is always initiated by man. The Jews modified this perspective when they placed their feasts in a historical context. This meant that the rite was now connected with history, and salvation history is the result of God's gratuitous interventions. More importance is therefore to be accorded to the divine initiative.

A second step was taken when the prophets, defining the attitude of soul needed for the celebration of one feast or another, decided that this attitude is God's gift, and it cannot exist or be maintained in us without Him. He must change our hearts of stone into hearts of flesh. Then the rite can become a channel of divine grace. It will not merely commemorate an act of God, it will be an act of God.

But the final step was reached when Christ Himself appeared to His apostles on a Sunday. It was no longer man who chose the day for worship. It was the Father—and the Son who manifested Himself on that day—who made this choice. It was no longer primarily a day on which man turned towards his god, but a day of which God manifested Himself to man. So we see that it was necessary to be strictly selective and to accept only those feasts that could be related to this divine manifestation. This was a difficult decision because the feasts had become encrusted with all the additions made by men who believed that their celebrations could in some way render service to God.

J. UNTIL HE RETURN

When Jewish law had made the feast a memorial of the past, and then recognized it as the celebration of a present liberation, it was easy for the prophets to show that it was also the expression of a hoped-for future. Most especially, after the Exile, this eschatological tension controlled the observance of Jewish feasts. The tabernacle in which the Lord had dwelt in the temple had been destroyed, so the feast of Tents now pointed to the future coming of the messiah, and was an anticipated celebration of the day when the messiah would come again to live in this tabernacle. This explains why Peter, when he recognized Jesus as the Messiah-God at the moment of the transfiguration, offered to erect for Him a tent.

The juiblee year, with its moratorium on debts, became more and more a type of the messianic era or the time of unending grace. Not until the assembly of a people divided by schism was it possible to look forward to a convocation in which all the tribes would meet in harmony and to foresee the day on which all nations would be one. The new-moon feasts were also a reminder that creation would one day know a new rhythm in which there would be a new heaven and a new earth.

Christ and the Church had no desire to be false to this eschatological dynamism. Just as the feast of Tents was privileged to provide the elements of the heavenly liturgy, so too would the New Year inaugurate an eternal era. Even now the observances of Sunday establish the rhythm of the last days and the Christian feast makes available messianic blessings. Each time that the Christian community assembles, it does so in expectation of the One who is to come, not only in the ceremonies which veil His Person, but also in the full manifestation of the powers He has shared with men.

K. CONCLUSION

It is obvious that a man-made rite must meet many conditions before it can become a Christian rite. As we reach the conclusion of this investigation, it is not surprising to discover that Sunday is the only feast that meets all these conditions. It alone possesses all the powers of the ancient feasts and brings them to full fruition when the Lord is in the midst of His people. He alone can officially convoke the final assembly of those who are saved. He alone can distribute messianic blessings in all their fullness. He alone can teach us how to act like God's children. If the feasts of the Passover and Pentecost both became part of the Christian liturgy, it is only insofar as they are related to Sunday. If the Church has adopted days of fast similar to those observed by the Jews, it is only because they have a place in a week that is always orientated to Sunday.

Perhaps our understanding of Christian feasts will deepen as a result of our investigation. We shall accustom ourselves to see in our feasts something more than simple rites. They will bring us, on the contrary, to an assembly of nomads who are never satisfied with this world and so are always journeying to heaven. Thanks to the Word that is proclaimed in these feasts they make us part of God's plan; they exact from us a very definite attitude of soul; above all else, they place at the center of our lives the mystery of Christ's Person both in His death and in His life.

It is possible that we could transfer in this way some contemporary pagan customs, purifying them so that, after they have gone through all the stages of the Jewish rites and feasts, they can signify the mystery of the Lord Himself. If we can do this, we shall have helped the pagan to purify himself so that he can share in the liturgy of the Church and discover the deep meaning of our Christian rites.